An Illustrated History of
Thailand

An Illustrated History of
Thailand

John Hoskin

JOHN BEAUFOY PUBLISHING

ASIA BOOKS

Published and distributed in Thailand by Asia Books Co., Ltd.
Berli Jucker House, 14th Floor, 99 Soi Rubia, Sukhumvit 42 Road,
Phrakanong, Klongtoey, Bangkok 10110, Thailand
Tel: (66) 2-715-9000; Fax: (66) 2-715-9197
Email: information@asiabooks.com
www.asiabooks.com

This edition published in the United Kingdom in 2018 by John Beaufoy Publishing,
11 Blenheim Court, 316 Woodstock Road, Oxford OX2 7NS, England
www.johnbeaufoy.com

ISBN 978-1-912081-88-2

Design: Glyn Bridgewater
Cartography: William Smuts
Editing and index: Krystyna Mayer
Project management: Rosemary Wilkinson

Printed and bound in Malaysia by Times Offset (M) Sdn. Bhd.

Pages 2–3: Mon craftsmanship exemplified in statuary and stucco work
at Wat Chama Thevi, Lamphun.

Page 5: A monk removes festive decoration from the *chedi*
at Wat Phra That Chom Kitti, Chiang Saen.

Page 6–7: The architectural splendour of Wat Mahathat at Sukhothai,
the nation's first sovereign capital.

CONTENTS

1

DEFINING THAILAND
Diversity and Unity

Thailand is situated at the heart of mainland Southeast Asia. Historically, it has drawn definition from its geographical position and from the religious, political, cultural and social ideas and institutions of its forerunners and neighbouring states. In turn, the early historical development of Southeast Asia as a whole was influenced by China and India, the two greatest ancient civilizations that bound the region east and west. As a result of these factors, modern Thailand is a multicultural society whose civilization has been forged between indigenous peoples and ethnic Tai, along with other immigrant groups, including Indian and Chinese. That said, the nation has evolved in such an individual way that 'Thainess' has been coined in modern usage to describe what is a unique culture and national identity (a product of both cultural realities and the kind of self-mythologizing found in most societies).

In common with many nations, Thailand has drawn widely on diverse external influences in fashioning its characteristic culture. This is true for the peoples of virtually all of Southeast Asia, who from the earliest times have adopted and adapted aspects of other cultures in the making of their own, while preserving their autonomy, but it is the Thais who have proved exceptionally adept as this kind of cultural osmosis.

There is thus enormous diversity in Thailand's make-up, but at the same time the nation has pursued a unity, even separateness, in its evolution. The pattern of development in many ways parallels that seen throughout mainland Southeast Asia. In this region fertile river valleys provided the environmental conditions for rice cultivation, which supported the rise of social units with governments in the hands of an elite, and social dynamics characterized by a recognized hierarchy rooted in patronage. However, Thailand's history differs from, say, the turbulence of rival kingdoms in Myanmar's past, or the fall of a high ancient civilization into centuries of obscurity as happened in the case of the Khmer of Cambodia. Most

OPPOSITE
Map of Thailand showing present-day borders and its strategic location at the heart of mainland Southeast Asia.

distinctive of all, Thailand was never colonized by a Western power as were all neighbouring countries without exception, and national pride in independence is characteristic of Thais. (Some might argue that Thailand colonized itself by having Western advisers and adopting Western ways, though this is scarcely comparable to the imposition of colonial rule.)

Allied with the Thais' acute awareness of their distinct and independent cultural identity is a popular consciousness of a continuity of historical development in which myth is mingled with fact. Exemplary of an imaginative historical consciousness is the *Ramakien*, the national epic that is Thailand's equivalent of the *Odyssey*. A variant of the Indian *Ramayana* composed from oral traditions more than 2,000 years ago, the *Ramakien* is Thai. Bas reliefs and other archaeological evidence suggest that the story was well known as early as the Sukhothai period, and it is likely that various local texts were produced at different times (although the oldest surviving text is that of King Rama I, composed in 1798).

LEFT
Thammasat University students in a performance of Khon, a masked dance dramatization of the Ramakien that was first developed in the 16th century.

OPPOSITE
A scene from the Ramakien, the national epic that has had a pervasive influence on all forms of Thai classical art and is here depicted in a mural at Bangkok's Wat Phra Kaeo.

So persuasive has been the *Ramakien*'s influence that the story informs virtually all classical Thai art, from dance drama to mural painting. A moral tale that relates the story of Prince Rama's struggles against the forces of evil, the *Ramakien* is familiar as both literature and poetic history that has links with fact. For instance, Ayutthaya, the Thai capital from 1351 to 1767, was almost certainly named after Prince Rama's city of Ayodhya, while the reigning Chakri dynasty has adopted 'Rama' as a regal title.

In spite of Thailand's sense of unity and continuity, the country's historical progression has been complex. The foundations of national identity – religion and monarchy in particular – were established in the earliest days of statehood dating back to the 13th century. However, it is only in comparatively recent times that all elements – social, political, cultural and linguistic – have cohered into what is recognizable today as Thai and Thailand. The current national borders date from the late 19th and early 20th centuries, and only in the last 200 years has the Thai language been standardized, although regional dialects still differ to a degree. The country's name was adopted as late as 1939, when 'Thailand', a fabricated word, replaced the previous name of 'Siam' (the term *syam* is first mentioned in a 12th-century Khmer inscription, where it refers to vassals of the Angkor Empire).

The course of Thai history is therefore one of change within a broad context of continuity, as different peoples, indigenous and immigrant, have interacted and shaped the institutions that have come to define the nation state. Within that structure, Buddhism and monarchy are the principal cornerstones. This was re-emphasized in 1917, when the country adopted a new tricolour national flag in which the red, white and blue represent the Thai nation, Buddhism and the monarchy respectively.

BUDDHISM

Animists in the distant past of prehistory, the Thais adopted Theravada Buddhism as their national religion when they first achieved statehood in the 13th century AD and have consistently adhered to the faith. Today approximately 94 per cent of the population professes and practises Buddhism, which is considered a badge of national identity. It is constitutionally stipulated that the Thai monarch be a Buddhist and protector of the faith, although in keeping with Buddhism's essential tolerance other religions have freedom of practice.

Founded in the 6th century BC in northern India as an offshoot of Brahmanism and Hinduism, Buddhism progressed quickly and extensively. Nevertheless, divisions appeared in the monkhood a century after the death of the religion's founder, Gautama Siddhartha, eventually resulting in the establishment of different sects, the two principal forms being Theravada and Mahayana Buddhism. Although both these schools hold much in common there is a fundamental difference in the emphasis each places on aspects of the Buddha's teachings and religious training. Essentially, Theravada Buddhism stresses the importance of monastic discipline in the development of higher spirituality as originally formulated in the Pali scriptures, whereas Mahayana Buddhism uses a Sanskrit version of the teachings and is more liberal and flexible in the interpretation of doctrine and practice.

When and how Buddhism arrived in what is now Thailand is a matter of debate among scholars. Archaeological evidence suggests that various forms of the religion were introduced at different periods before the ascendency of the Thais. Some historians hold that Buddhism reached Thailand as early as the 3rd century BC, when the Indian emperor Asoka (*c.* 274–232 BC), a Buddhist convert, sent missionaries to various territories in Asia. According to evidence in ancient Sri Lankan chronicles, one of these was known as Suvarnabhumi, meaning 'Golden Land'. Opinions differ over the exact location of Suvarnabhumi, although it seems probable that it extended over an area at present defined by southern Myanmar, central Thailand and eastern Cambodia.

Various sites have been proposed as the territory's cultural centre, one contender being Nakhon Pathom, west of present-day Bangkok, which much later was an important religious hub for the Mon peoples whose Dvaravati kingdom flourished in central Thailand from the 6th to the 11th centuries AD. The religious significance of Nakhon Pathom persists today in Phra Pathom Chedi, the world's tallest Buddhist monument, with a height of 127 metres (417 feet), which was constructed in the mid-19th century over a ruined monument believed to date back to the 6th century.

The Buddhism of Asoka was of the early Theravada school, while forms of the religion entering Thailand during the first centuries AD differed in belonging predominantly to the Mahayana sect, with a strong mix of Brahmanism and Hinduism. In southern Thailand evidence in the form of *chedis* and images of both the Buddha and Bodhisattvas (future Buddhas), found notably at Chaiya and Nakhon Si Thammarat, indicate that Mahayana Buddhism was prevalent when the area was under the control of the Sumatra-based Kingdom of Srivijaya (8th–13th centuries).

In the 11th century what is now central Thailand came under the dominance of Angkor, and archaeological finds at major Khmer outposts such as Lopburi again show Mahayana influences, together with a pronounced Hindu element. It was at this time that various groups of Tai peoples were moving into the region from their homeland in southern China and gradually accepted Theravada Buddhism, mostly likely from the Mon.

By the early 13th century, petty Tai states became strong enough to supplant the Khmer and establish their own kingdom at Sukhothai where, as recorded in a stone inscription accredited to the third monarch, King Ramkhamhaeng (*c.* 1279–1298), Theravada Buddhism was adopted as the national religion. This represented a clear departure from the past, with the form of Thai Buddhism established at Sukhothai adhering to a 'pure' tradition that had become rooted in Sri Lanka after Buddhism's decline in India, and received in Thailand via successive visits by Sri Lankan monks.

Although Sri Lankan Theravada Buddhism continued to be and remains a defining element of Thai identity, some influences of Brahmanism, inherited from the Khmer, have been retained, especially in royal ceremonies. Traces of the animism of the Thai's ancestors also persist in popular belief, most readily witnessed in the spirit houses found in the compound of virtually every business, government and domestic building. None of these extraneous influences,

OPPOSITE
Wat Phra Mahathat at Nakhon Si Thammarat is believed to date back more than a thousand years and attests to the early importance of Buddhism in what is now southern Thailand.

BELOW
Lopburi in the Central Plains was an important regional hub during various periods, notably a second capital for King Narai in the 17th century, as witnessed by the imposing ruins of the residence of his Greek advisor, Constantine Phaulkon.

however, contradicts Theravada Buddhism, a non-theistic religion. Its vitality today is inescapable, not only in the huge number of Buddhist temples seen throughout the country, but also in the persistence of such traditional customs as monks making early morning alms rounds, and the practice of young men entering the monkhood for at least a brief period once in their lives.

MONARCHY

Kingship has always defined the Thai state and continues to do so. The concept has at times changed, but like Theravada Buddhism, to which there are close bonds, monarchy underpins Thailand's historical development. Thai history has traditionally been told in terms of the action of kings, and the monarchy is unmistakably paramount in any understanding of that history.

The Thai monarchy was established at Sukhothai, the first unified Thai state, by its founder King Si Indraditya (*c.* 1238–1270s). The nature of kingship was inherited from the Khmer, whom the Thais supplanted, and was based on two concepts taken respectively from Hinduism and Theravada Buddhism. One was the Hindu caste of *Kshatriya*, or warrior-king, who ruled by right of military power. The other was the Theravada Buddhist idea of *Dhammaraja*, whereby a king's rule should be in accord with the teachings of the Buddha, the *Dhamma*.

These concepts were abandoned briefly during the reign of the third Sukhothai monarch, King Ramkhamhaeng, who introduced a paternalistic model in which the king ruled as a father over his children. As recorded in the stone inscription accredited to this reign (see page 47), the monarchy was approachable by all to receive petitions and settle disputes.

After Sukhothai was supplanted by the younger Thai Kingdom of Ayutthaya, founded in 1351, the two earlier Khmer-inherited concepts of monarchy were re-established along with a third, that of *Dhevaraja*, or Divine-King (the association of the sovereign with the divine). In this the monarch is believed to be a reincarnation of the god Vishnu, as well as being a Bodhisattva (future Buddha), thereby having religious and moral authority as well as legitimacy by the right of birth. As *Dhevaraja* was derived from Brahmanism, Brahmin priests came to play a central role in royal rites, while the king, as a semi-divine figure, became an object of veneration to his subjects. The monarchy was absolute and kings were known as 'Lords of Life', remaining largely remote from the people. The question of succession and the concept of a legitimist line remained ill defined until modern times. In the mid-15th century King Trailok of Ayutthaya introduced the position of *Uparaja*, or Deputy King, in an attempt to regulate succession. The position was not necessarily attained by primogeniture, although full brothers or sons were usually made *Uparaja*, but even then succession was not a clear-cut matter, and usurpation was common.

Following the sacking of Ayutthaya at the hands of the Burmese in 1767, Bangkok was established as the capital in 1782 and the current Chakri dynasty was founded under King Phra Phutthayotfa, Rama I (1782–1809). The Ayutthaya model of kingship was maintained, although with increasing moves to modernize the state along Western lines, especially under King Chulalongkorn, Rama V (1868–1910), the monarchy became more 'enlightened' while at the same time remaining absolute.

That changed with the bloodless revolution of 1932, led by foreign-educated students and military officers whose demands for a constitution were accepted (with reluctance) by King Prajadhipok, Rama VII (1925–1935). Absolute monarchy was thus ended and ever since the role of the king has been that of a symbolic head of state, although certain powers have been retained, such as the prerogative of royal assent and the power of pardon. Nonetheless, the king remains highly revered by the people, and even though he lacks executive powers he is much more than a mere figurehead, serving as a unifying and exemplary force for the well-being of the people.

The huge popular respect in which the Thai monarchy is held makes it exceptional among present-day constitutional monarchies (and the late King Bhumibol Adulyadej, Rama IX, who died in October 2016 at the age of 88, was further noteworthy as the longest reigning of all still-serving heads of state). Such is the reverence that the law of lese-majesty (each constitution since 1932 has maintained the king as 'enthroned in a position of revered worship and shall [sic] not be violated') continues to be exercised, although misuse (or overuse), typically as a way to discredit political opponents, has led to controversy in the 21st century and there have been calls to modify, though not abolish, the law.

ORIGINS OF THE THAI

Thailand has a population made up of various ethnic groups, including the Mon and Khmer of pre-Thai civilizations, as well as Chinese, Indian and other later arrivals, although the majority is Tai. This is a generic term applied to a people identified as belonging to a specific cultural and linguistic group spread widely across mainland Southeast Asia and today found predominantly in Thailand. Every citizen of the modern nation is 'Thai', but the roots of that identity lie in the history of the Tai.

There is no consensus on the origin of the Tai. Among recent theories, for example, is the suggestion that the Tai originated in Thailand and subsequently spread to other parts of the region, including China. This theory is based on the prehistoric finds made at Ban Chiang in the present-day Thai province of Udon Thani in the north-east of the country; according to some archaeologists they point to a bronze metallurgy culture dating back 3,500 years. Even so, there is no way of knowing whether or not the people of that culture were Tai.

ABOVE
Postage stamps issued during the reign of King Prajadhipok, Rama VII (1925-1935). The founding of Thailand's Postal Department dates back to 1881.

Other arguments claim that the Tai were originally Austronesian rather than Mongoloid, but the standard theory holds to roots in prehistoric mainland Southeast Asia, a fertile, thickly forested and biodiverse area. Historian David K. Wyatt describes a 'Southeast Asian pool, or heartland, located perhaps in the extreme northern portions of Southeast Asia and in central and southern China', where perhaps as far back as 40,000 years ago hunter-gatherers in the region were settling in relatively permanent sites. Evolving over the millennia among what was at first a sparse population were the domestication of animals such as cattle and fowl, rice cultivation and metal working. Not until about 10,000 years ago did individual ethnic groups, which were differentiated linguistically and culturally, spread over a broad area from the Yangtze Valley in central China to the Indonesian archipelago.

LEFT
Thailand inaugurated a Banknotes Department in 1902 and these second series issue notes, current during the reign of King Rama VII, have a guilloche design with 12 rays on the front and on the back an illustration of the Royal Ploughing Ceremony.

19

The first recorded Chinese references to the Tai date from the 6th century BC and mention a people who lived in river valleys and subsisted on wet rice cultivation supplemented by fishing. It is presumed that the group of languages known as Tai originated amongst these people, who inhabited the region south of the Yangtze River before the arrival of the Han Chinese from the north in the 6th century BC. Over the next several centuries the Chinese became organized as an empire with a powerful emperor, while the Tais remained divided into small groups each ruled by a chieftain. To avoid being absorbed by the Chinese the Tais had only the alternative of mass migration if they were to maintain their independence.

In the early centuries AD, growing pressure from the Chinese and Vietnamese probably increased the migration of groups of Tais from what is today China's Yunnan province to Southeast Asia; they followed the rivers and valleys that ran south and spread widely throughout the region as far west as Assam in northeast India. This 'great trek', as HRH Prince Chula Chakrabongse describes it in his *Lords of Life: A History of the Kings of Thailand*, was slow, taking hundreds of years, and still the Tais remained in small separate groups under their own individual leaders.

It is open to question how far the powerful militaristic kingdom of Nanchao, which emerged in the 8th century AD in Yunnan with an economy based on rice cultivation and bronze casting, was a Tai state. It certainly harboured a multi-ethnic population that included Tais, although they were unlikely to have been part of any ruling elite. It is more probable that Nanchao accepted independent Tai states that arose just beyond its southern border in the 11th and 12th centuries. Nanchao was significant, however, in that it blocked Chinese influence from the north and thus protected Tai groups that had not already migrated from being assimilated into the Chinese cultural sphere. It can also be assumed that Nanchao stimulated Tai expansion and migration, which would have been greatly accelerated by the invading Mongol armies of Kublai Khan in the 13th century.

Certainly by the 13th century, in what seems a general pattern of occupation of broad river basins and foothills, distinct settled groupings of Tais had become differentiated as the Shan in Myanmar, as the Lao in the upper Mekong River Basin and as various tribal units in present-day northern Vietnam. Many others

settled in the Chao Phraya River Basin on the western edge of the then Angkor Empire, where the Tai language that was the precursor to the national language of modern Thailand eventually became dominant.

The original inhabitants of the land into which the Tais moved were possibly aboriginal forest tribes, though these had mostly been replaced by more cultural-ly accomplished peoples – Burmese, Mon, Khmer and Lawa – before the arrival of the Tai, with the Mon and the Khmer evolving as the dominant civilizations respectively to the west and east. As they grew in numbers and became more settled, the Tai were influenced by the various groups with which they came into contact and, as historian D. G. E. Hall so aptly put it, 'they were as remarkable as assimilators as the Normans in Europe'.

The Chao Phraya, Thailand's major river, has historically been the country's main communications artery and its river basin was the principal area of early Tai settlement.

2

BEFORE THE THAI
Early Civilizations
Prehistory to the 12th century AD

The land that now encompasses Thailand and its neighbours has a long history of human habitation dating back to the Neolithic era. Some theories even identify the region as one of the cradles of civilization with cultures adept in agriculture and metallurgy. While no definitive picture is possible, climate, geography and the archaeological evidence that has been brought to light give some indication of development before recorded history.

THE ENVIRONMENT AND EARLY HUMAN SETTLEMENT

Geographically, mainland Southeast Asia is defined by great river systems divided roughly north to south by mountain ranges. Thailand's principal river is the Chao Phraya, which is formed by the confluence of four rivers – the Ping, Wang, Yom and Nan – that flow through the north of the country and unite near the town of Nakhon Sawan, from where the Chao Phraya runs south to empty into the Gulf of Thailand just below Bangkok. Hills and mountain ranges separate the country from China to the north, and from Myanmar and Cambodia in the west and south-east respectively, while in the east the Mekong River forms the border with Laos. This geographical formation fostered the rise of a civilization that, while sharing influences with its neighbours, was sufficiently separated to allow the development of its own distinct language and culture.

Supporting human habitation was a natural environment that was extremely fertile and densely forested, conditions that in the prehistoric period sustained small groups of hunter-gatherers. Indeed, the forests with their abundance of food in the Chao Phraya Valley, in central Thailand, may have delayed a move beyond a hunting and gathering economy, whereas in the highland valleys to the north rice cultivation, and hence a more settled social and political unit, appeared early, perhaps around the 4th millennium BC.

OPPOSITE
Present-day view of the Kok River at Tha Thon, northern Thailand. Such fertile upland valleys provided both migratory routes and areas of early settlement as the Tai gradually moved southwards from Yunnan.

Forests and rivers also helped to define cultural practices, with wood and bamboo being the preferred materials for domestic dwellings, and houses being raised on stilts to provide protection from floods and wild animals. Water from the rivers was utilized for wet-rice cultivation. Rice was the staple food and was supplemented by fish rather than meat (there would have been no grazing livestock due to the absence of grasslands). Rivers would also have served as transportation links.

A picture of a typical Tai settlement during the first millennium AD, drawn from scant evidence and largely from accounts by their neighbours rather than the Tai themselves, shows a sparse landscape dotted with scattered villages of farming households separated by tracts of forest and mountain ranges. Such villages would not have been totally self-sustaining and would have been dependent to some extent on trade for basic commodities such as salt and metal. They were also vulnerable to raids by bandits.

THE TAI SOCIAL UNIT

Over time villages evolved into what became the basic Tai social and political unit, the *mueang*, a term difficult to translate but in essence describing an embryonic city-state. In the highland river valleys where the Tais first settled, a *mueang* was a fortified town around which a number of villages clustered for mutual benefit and defence.

As the Tais continued their south-westerly migration into the lowlands, *mueang* were developed along rivers, typically at a bend where a canal could be cut to form a protective moat (a pattern that was widely adopted later, when major cities and towns were built after the founding of the Thai nation). Coastal settlements differed largely in that they relied more on sea trade than agriculture as the main means of livelihood.

Ruling over the *mueang* was a *chao*, or lord, whose authority arose from personal qualities and was sustained by a system of patronage. Initially a *chao* probably acted as a sort of landlord, ordering land management and agricultural production, but as settle-ments grew the local lord became more effectively a ruler whose resources could perhaps include an army. In return for the chao's protection, villagers were indebted to provide labour service or perhaps a tax in the form of agricultural produce. In time a social hierarchy would probably have evolved, whereby early settlers formed an elite over later arrivals.

At first the *mueang* was a relatively small entity with only a very few settlements expanding into larger units. Not until the 13th century do ambitious Tai rulers appear bent on expanding their power and spheres of influence. Moreover, it was an insecure world and settle-ments were frequently moved and re-sited due to out-breaks of war or disease.

What is particularly important about the *mueang* is that it fostered cooperation and the efficient use of manpower, as well as a functional social order under an effective leadership, even though the latter was to an extent unstable due to its reliance on purely personal qualities.

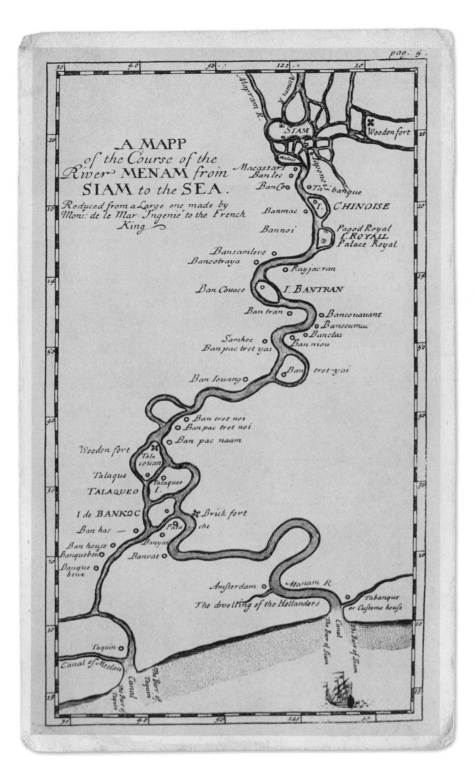

An early map of the Chao Phraya (identified by its original name of menam, which simply means 'river'), the course of which largely dictated the development of Tai civilization, the waterway being both a source of irrigation and a transportation link.

BAN CHIANG

Civilization in the area that Thailand now encompasses stretches far back into prehistory, and while traces are few, excavations at Ban Chiang, on the Khorat Plateau near the modern town of Udon Thani in north-eastern Thailand, put the area firmly on the map of prehistoric development.

THE DISCOVERY OF BAN CHIANG

Ban Chiang is considered to be the most important prehistoric settlement in Southeast Asia, and the archaeological digs, begun in the 1960s, have unearthed burial grounds dating back to around 2100 BC. The finds provide the earliest evidence of farming, pottery making and metalworking in the region. The location is today preserved as a World Heritage Site, and one excavation pit has been left open to show the scale of the dig, although it is the adjacent museum housing archaeological finds, especially finely crafted and distinctively patterned pottery, that affords a better insight into the significance of the discovery.

LEFT AND OPPOSITE
Preserved today as a museum, the archaeological site of Ban Chiang, on the Khorat Plateau, is the region's most important prehistoric settlement with evidence of a civilization dating back at least 4,000 years.

The Khorat Plateau was probably first settled in around 3600 BC by an indigenous people who successfully developed their way of life from hunter-gathering to sedentary farming. Subsequently, between *c.* 1000 and *c.* 500 BC, agriculture was advanced with the introduction of wet-rice cultivation, along with more refinement in ceramic and metal production. As evidenced by grave goods, this was also a time of considerable prosperity and, with human remains showing few signs of violent death, a period of relative peace. Further social and technological refinement was achieved in the late Ban Chiang period, from *c.* 500 BC to AD 200–300, most vividly witnessed in sophisticated pottery decorated with distinctive whirl designs.

Ban Chiang seems to have been abandoned in the 3rd century, although settlement continued at other sites in the area. The particular significance of the archaeological discovery was that it proved settlement by an indigenous people who were independent of external influences from either India or China, which before the Ban Chiang finds were thought to have been the stimulus for cultural development in the region.

FUNAN

Although evidence is sketchy, the earliest and most important true state to emerge in Southeast Asia was Funan, which is assumed to have risen to prominence in the 1st century AD in the Lower Mekong Valley and Delta, in present-day Cambodia and southern Vietnam. Funan's territory did not encompass land that is now part of Thailand, and its significance to Thai history is in the influence it had on succeeding states in mainland Southeast Asia.

Apart from some archaeological evidence, knowledge of the civilization is derived from Chinese records, in particular the accounts of two Chinese emissaries from the Wu Emperor, Kang Dai and Zhu Ying, who visited Funan in the 3rd century AD. Even the name of the kingdom comes from the Chinese, with French scholar Georges Coedes believing it to be a transliteration of the Khmer word *bnam* (*phnom* in modern Khmer), meaning 'mountain', although there is no evidence that this was the name used by the people of Funan. Similarly, the ethnolinguistic make-up of the Funanese is unclear. The most widely held theories are that the majority of the population was either Mon-Khmer or Austronesian, or that the society was multi-ethnic in nature.

According to legend Funan was founded by an Indian Brahman named Kaundinya, who was guided to the area by a dream and there threw a sacred javelin to mark the site of Funan's capital Vyadhapura. Here he is assumed to have founded a dynasty by marrying Soma, the daughter of the Naga king, a local native chief.

The generally held view is that the development of early kingdoms in

Southeast Asia was stimulated by increasing political and cultural contact with Indian travellers and merchants engaged in the sea trade with China in a process that has been termed 'Indianization' (though a more recent argument is the idea of 'localization'). The degree of 'Indianization' – whether its imported ideas of kingship and other concepts actually fostered local kingdoms or merely strengthened and legitimized existing power structures – is currently a matter of debate among historians. It seems clear, however, that Funan followed the pattern of an Indian kingdom ruled by a maharaja and exerting control over surrounding vassal states. It was this model of kingship that would be of particular significance in the rise of later states, including those of the Thai, which evolved as the *chao* of an expanding *mueang* sought to make himself a *raja* and establish *a ratcha (raja)-anacak,* or kingdom.

While acknowledging that aspects of everyday life, such as houses typically built on stilts and customs like cock-fighting, were indigenous and unaffected by Indianization, Coedes has written that:

> It was from India that the cultured section of Funanese society acquired their religion, their burial customs, their art, their writing as found from the 3rd century onwards, their knowledge of Sanskrit, and no doubt many features of their material culture, in particular their highly developed irrigation system.

According to Chinese sources Funan was a single socio-political unit, although some historians today suggest that it was a collection of city-states that were sometimes united and at other times in conflict. Whatever is the case, Funan probably held sway over the Indochina peninsula for five centuries, with its wealth derived from maritime trade and its sizeable population sustained by abundant rice cultivation in the fertile Mekong Delta.

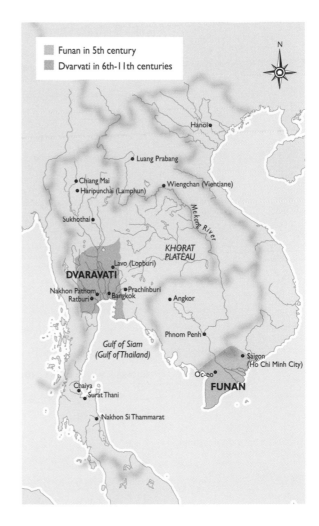

Funan in 5th century
Dvarvati in 6th–11th centuries

N

Hanoi

Luang Prabang

Chiang Mai
Haripunchai (Lamphun)

Wiengchan (Vientiane)

Sukhothai

Mekong River

KHORAT PLATEAU

Lavo (Lopburi)

DVARAVATI

Nakhon Pathom
Ratburi
Bangkok

Prachinburi

Angkor

Phnom Penh

Gulf of Siam
(Gulf of Thailand)

Saigon
(Ho Chi Minh City)

Oc-eo

FUNAN

Chaiya
Surat Thani

Nakhon Si Thammarat

Excavations at Oc-eo, Funan's mercantile centre located on the west coast of the Mekong Delta, have revealed a walled seaport and a finely engineered network of canals that would have provided links with other settlements in the kingdom, while archaeological finds have included Roman, Persian, Indian and Chinese artefacts. All the evidence shows Funan to have been a powerful commercial force that benefited from its location on the trade route that linked China to India, beyond to the Middle East and ultimately to the Mediterranean.

Before AD 350, Indian merchants sailed across the Gulf of Bengal to the Kra Isthmus, in what is now southern Thailand, and from there overland to the Gulf of Thailand (travelling along various routes such as that running between the once coastal town of Trang, later relocated to its present inland site, and the archaeological site of Chaiya). Ships would then skirt around the rim of the Gulf to Oc-eo, where they would wait for favourable winds to take them on up the Vietnamese coast to China.

Chinese travellers recorded that the people of Funan were dark and curly haired, and 'lived in walled cities, palaces and houses'. They were skilled artisans, producing gold and silver jewellery, and although the ordinary people were engaged primarily in agriculture, the elite was literate, used Sanskrit and kept archives, and there was a legal system involving trial by ordeal, such as carrying red-hot chains or plunging hands into boiling water. Overall, the Chinese regarded the Funanese as a relatively sophisticated people (in spite of pirate attacks on their merchant junks) and, notably, a group of musicians who visited China in the mid-3rd century AD was amicably received.

Funan reached the peak of its power in the 3rd century AD under the leadership of King Fan Shiman, who expanded his navy and successfully attacked neighbouring kingdoms which, according to Chinese accounts, 'all acknowledged themselves his vassals'. Given Funan's location and maritime power, it is probable that it came to exert some degree of political control over all the city-states along the eastern coast of peninsular Thailand, as well as down the Malay peninsula.

Following a shift in the sea route of India-China trade in the latter half of the 4th century, when shipping travelled further south to the islands of Java and Sumatra, so bypassing the Kra Isthmus land crossing, Funan's power began to wane and the kingdom was eventually eclipsed in the 6th century AD by the Khmer state of Chen-la, the forerunner of Angkor. Its legacy, however, was considerable. Funan had accelerated the process of Indianization in mainland Southeast Asia, and established political, social and economic patterns that would influence future states in the region.

DVARAVATI

A conglomeration of city-states known collectively as Dvaravati formed the earliest established settlements in central Thailand. The majority of the population was probably Mon, members of the Mon-Khmer linguistic group, although there is some evidence from sculptures that Dvaravati society included other ethnic groups, possibly Khmer and Malay. Originally from south-west China, groups of Mon migrated down the Irrawaddy Valley and the Ping River Valley. They settled respectively in lower Myanmar and in Thailand's Chao Phraya River Basin, where they founded a collection of principalities that were to hold sway over the region from the 6th – some historians speculate an earlier date – to the 11th centuries AD.

The period is, however, problematic, Dvaravati being somewhat enigmatic with little being known of its history, geographical extent and political constitution, nor whether it had a single capital. Principal among Dvaravati's cities appears to have been Nakhon Pathom, 56 kilometres (35 miles) west of present-day Bangkok, where a coin was found with the inscription 'Lord of Dvaravati', the only known local reference to the name. The word 'Dvaravati' is derived from the Pali *Nagara Pathama*, which translates as 'First City', and Nakhon Pathom is usually considered the earliest city in Thailand, most likely founded in the 6th century AD, although some historians suggest that it may date back to the 3rd century BC, when it was visited by Indian Buddhist missionaries.

At this time Nakhon Pathom was a port city and only later was the coastline pushed back due to the Chao Phraya River's sedimentation. This would have given the settlement prominence on the India-China trade route, thus exposing it to external cultural influences.

Whether earlier or later, it does seem that the Mon were the first recipients of Theravada Buddhism in Thailand, and Nakhon Pathom was an important religious centre. Also, Mon craftsmen were highly skilled in stone sculpture, as well as stucco and terracotta architectural decoration, as attested

Carved stone Dhammachakra, Wheels of the Law, were widely produced by Dvaravati craftsmen. Influenced by Indian styles, the symbol represents the ever-turning doctrine of the Buddha set in motion by his first sermon preached at the Deer Park at Sarnath, India.

*Wat Chama Thevi at
Haripunchai (present-day
Lamphun) is one of the
few surviving examples
of Dvaravati religious
architecture, believed to have
been built in the 8th or
9th century and subsequently
restored several times.*

OPPOSITE
*Wat Haripunchai is reputed
to have been founded in
1044 on the site of the
palace of Queen Chama
Thevi, the legendary founder
of the northern Dvaravati
kingdom, although the
chedi pictured here is a
15th-century construction in
the Lanna style.*

in a number of Buddha images, votive tablets and other finds, with many of the ancient images showing influences of Indian Gupta and post-Gupta styles.

Nakhon Pathom and other Dvaravati sites were clustered around the edge of the Chao Phraya River Basin; they include Ratburi to the south-west, Lavo (Lopburi) to the north and Prachinburi in the east. From this core Dvaravati also extended eastwards across the Khorat Plateau and into the far north at Haripunchai (Lamphun), which is thought to have been founded by a group of emigrants from Lavo led by the legendary Queen Chama Thevi in the 8th century.

Dvaravati fell into decline in the 11th century, with most cities falling to the Khmer in their expansion westwards from their capital at Angkor, in Cambodia. Haripunchai, however, continued as an independent city-state, successfully holding out against several Khmer sieges in the 11th century, and enjoyed a late golden age until its defeat by the Tais of the Lanna kingdom in 1281. Before that, in the late Dvaravati period, it is likely that the Tais were moving into the region in greater numbers, co-existing with the Mon and absorbing certain social and cultural elements but not yet dominating.

SRIVIJAYA

Coexistent with the period of Dvaravati's domination in the Chao Phraya River Basin was Srivijaya influence over the primordial Malay city-states in southern peninsular Thailand that had earlier been vassals of Funan. With its capital at Palembang on the Indonesian island of Sumatra, Srivijaya was a maritime trading power that extended across the coastal areas of the Indonesian archipelago, the Malay peninsula and southern Thailand between the 8th and 13th centuries. That, at least, is the general theory and, as is the case with Dvaravati, there is scant archaeological evidence to give any certainty as to whether Srivijaya was an empire with a capital city, or just a loose federation of various coastal settlements. It is improbable that Palembang was a major naval power, and instead it must have derived strength from being an intermediate port for trade, especially in spices, sandalwood and pearls, between India and China. As such it was the heir to Funan's earlier commercial monopoly. Srivijaya kings would most likely have exerted direct rule only in the capital, areas beyond being under the control of local chiefs, and even then influence was probably limited to coastal settlements without any significant penetration further inland.

CHAIYA

Archaeological evidence suggests that the Srivijayan empire's principal regional centre in Thailand was Chaiya, near present-day Surat Thani on the east coast of the southern peninsula. The name is thought to be a contraction of the word 'Srivijaya', and some Thai historians believe that the site was at one time the Srivijayan capital. This theory has by and large been discounted, but Chaiya was clearly a place of some importance, as evidenced by the now-restored *chedi* of Borom That Chaiya, which is a good example of the Srivijaya architectural style. Also discovered here was the superb bronze Avalokitesvara Bodhisattva, now in the National Museum in Bangkok, the sculpture particularly notable for being highly decorated with ornate jewellery.

As much as it was a commercial power, Srivijaya was an important centre for Mahayana Buddhist expansion between the 8th and 12th centuries, and a Chinese pilgrim visiting Palembang in the 7th century recorded that more than 1,000 Buddhist monks lived there. Some scholars believe it was Mahayana Buddhism rather than commerce that was Srivijaya's unifying force, and this common belief allowed the development of a distinctive artistic style (later classified as 'Srivijaya' by art historians). Certainly, in terms of its impact on southern Thailand, at Chaiya, Nakhon Si Thammarat and other coastal sites, Srivijaya religious art and architecture, stylistically influenced by India and central Java, significantly distinguishes the region's cultural development before the 13th century. Most especially achievements in stone sculpture and bronze casting were taken to new heights.

LEFT
A fine example of Srivijayan art, this 9th- or 10th-century bronze sculpture of Avalokitesvara (one of the Bodhisattva of Mahayana Buddhism) was discovered at Chaiya in what is now southern Thailand.

KHMER

The Khmer, like the Mon, had entered Southeast Asia along the migration route from southern China perhaps as early as the 9th century BC. While the Mon occupied the Central Plains and northern highlands of modern Thailand, along with large parts of Myanmar, the Khmer settled in the southern Mekong Valley. Here in AD 802 the Khmer King Jayavarman II founded the state of Angkor, last of the major pre-Tai civilizations and the one that had the greatest and most lasting influence on the eventual founding of a Thai sovereign state.

For six centuries Khmer civilization dominated mainland Southeast Asia. Basing its highly developed institutions on advanced Indian cultural concepts, Angkor evolved as a rich and complex civilization, with its art and architecture of an accomplishment comparable to that of Ancient Egypt and Greece. At the greatest extent of its influence in the 12th century, Angkor's control extended south to the Mekong Delta in present-day Vietnam, north into Laos and west over large tracts of what is now Thailand.

ANGKOR

The name 'Angkor' is derived from the Sanskrit word *nagara*, meaning 'city' or 'capital', and from Jayavarman II onwards, Khmer kings legitimized and symbolized their power by building a temple-mountain at the heart of their capital. The precise limits of this changed under various monarchs and the Angkor complex seen today comprises the remains of several successive cities, while the very earliest capitals stood a short distance away. Over nearly three centuries, up until the early 13th century, Angkor grew as successive monarchs built monuments to their lasting power and glory, monuments unsurpassed architecturally in mainland Southeast Asia.

After Suryavarman II (1113–1150), the Khmer faced increasingly troubled times. A succession of major and minor upsets culminated with the defeat of Angkor in 1177 by the Khmer's traditional enemies, the Chams, who won a decisive naval battle on the Tonle Sap (Great Lake). Ironically, out of this disaster was to rise Angkor's last great monarch, Jayavarman VII (1181–1219). A man of remarkable ability, he succeeded in expelling the Chams and not only reconstructed Angkor, but also embarked on an empire-wide building programme far more ambitious and more prolific in it projects than anything undertaken by his predecessors.

OPPOSITE
A stone statue of Khmer King Jayavarman VII inside Prasat Hin Phimai, on the Khorat Plateau, attests to the once dominance of the Khmer over areas that subsequently became part of the Tai world.

Although Angkor remained the centre of a viable empire for another two centuries, the death of Jayavarman VII was the beginning of the end. There was no more major building (or none that has survived), and in spite of continuing prosperity Angkor was effectively in decline. Increasingly, the Khmer were threatened by the emergent kingdom of the Thais to the west. Finally, in 1431, the Thais succeeded in defeating Angkor.

Unlike its predecessors, Funan and the later smaller state of Chen-la, located in the lower Mekong Valley and Delta, Angkor was a defined capital, a political and cultural heart that allowed the consolidation of what before the 800s AD were fragmented groups of Khmer living in the Lower Mekong Basin. Angkor also differed in that its power was derived from agriculture rather than international commerce. The city had an advantageous location close to the northwestern shore of the Tonle Sap, fed by the river of the same name, a tributary of the Mekong, which provided transport links that allowed control of land and labour resources. Moreover, the Khmer were not only master builders, as testified by Angkor Wat and the temples of Angkor Thom. They were also skilled in hydraulic engineering and mastered techniques of storing water in reservoirs (*barays*), and of building irrigation networks to control flooding and provide water for year-round multiple rice harvests.

There is further contrast with earlier so-called kingdoms in that clear historical references survive in numerous Khmer stone inscriptions. In what was a highly organized social hierarchy, the Khmer established the cult of *Dhevara-ja*, or 'god-king', which focused on worship of the linga of the Hindu god Siva, symbolizing the king's semi-divine ability to confer fertility and prosperity on his land and people (the royal suffix *varman* means 'protector'). The numerous temples built by the kings of Angkor, which on their deaths served as mausoleums, were designed to symbolize Mount Meru, the centre of the universe and realm of the gods, thus identifying the monarch with the divine world.

Supporting the cult of the god-king were Brahman priests who held an important position in the administrative hierarchy. Along with Siva, the Hindu god Vishnu and the Buddha also sanctified royal authority, and religious emphasis shifted at various times during the course of the empire's history. For example, Jayavarman VII favoured Mahayana Buddhism and built the Bayon, haunting with its multiple four-sided Buddha heads, as the symbol of his royal power.

With the centralized authority of its kings and the ability to mobilize labour on a large scale for both building works and military service, all supported by ample agricultural production, Angkor was able to pursue expansionist policies. Notably, in the early 11th century Suryavarman I extended Angkor's authority north and in particular west across Thailand's Central Plains.

At the empire's greatest extent, in the reign of Suryavarman II, it encompassed much of present-day Thailand, including the Khorat Plateau, where Phimai was a provincial hub, and the Chao Phraya Basin, with Lopburi an important centre, and extended west into Kanchanaburi, south to Phetburi and north to Phitsanulok, Sukhothai and Si Satchanalai on the upper edge of what are today Thailand's Central Plains. The ruling classes in these provincial areas were probably Khmer, with Khmer governors, some with royal connections, being appointed to exert authority over major regional outposts. However, in terms of total population the Khmer probably did not comprise the majority in the empire's outlying districts; there would have been concentrations of Mon, while growing numbers of Tai were steadily moving into the region.

ABOVE

Before the ascendancy of the Tai, Khmer influence extended over much of the territory now encompassed by Thailand. The legacy of the Khmer can be seen today in a number of temple ruins, of which Prasat Hin Phimai, dating from the late 10th and early 11th centuries, is a superb example.

KHMER ARCHITECTURAL LEGACY IN THAILAND

Traces of the Khmer in Thailand's cultural heritage are extensive and numerous temple ruins are widely distributed in Thailand, the largest concentration being on the Khorat Plateau. Many are comparable in their aesthetic and architectural achievements, if not in scale, to those of Angkor itself, and they suggest that what is now Thai territory was more than merely a provincial backwater. It is estimated, for example, that more than 300 stone temples were erected in the Mun River Valley alone. The principal surviving temple, Phimai, now preserved as a historical park, was linked to Angkor by a 225-kilometre (140-mile) 'Royal Way' punctuated by ornately decorated rest stations, each positioned a day's march from the next. Phimai is also notable for its distinctive corncob towers that slightly predate similar constructions at Angkor Wat.

During the reign of King Suryavarman II the limits of the empire were pushed to their furthest extremities with a series of military campaigns that included drives against the Mon, then the dominant people in the Chao Phraya River Valley. At this time Lavo was clearly more than a mere outpost of the Khmer empire, although its exact status is unclear; depending on how the later chronicles are interpreted, its ruler was either a Khmer governor or Suryavarman II himself.

Rising to power from a dynasty that was first established in the Mun Valley, Suryavarman II was the builder of Angkor Wat. The clearest picture of provincial importance can be found in the temple's bas reliefs. Depicted are parades of Khmer troops, including a contingent of Tai conscripts, named in an inscription as *Syam Kuk*, Siamese people, who are pictured as an ill-disciplined bunch, marching out of step. The troops from Lavo, however, are shown as completely Khmer in appearance and it can be presumed that at this time the Khmer did form the majority of the population in this area north of present-day Bangkok.

In spite of some periods of anarchy, when royal supremacy was weakened, the Khmer Empire was the dominant state in mainland Southeast Asia until entering into a protracted decline in the early 13th century. Angkor was finally abandoned in the 1430s after it was sacked by the Thai Kingdom of Ayutthaya, which in many respects became its cultural heir.

The Khmer influence on the rise of independent Thai states was not, however, immediate. As David K. Wyatt interestingly notes:

There are indications, from the way in which early Tai kingdoms seemed

OPPOSITE
Enigmatic stone faces looking to the four cardinal points top the gateways leading into Angkor Thom at the core of the ancient Khmer capital, which controlled much of mainland Southeast Asia from the 9th to the 15th centuries.

almost perversely to devise public institutions that contrasted sharply with Angkorian institutions, that Tai chafed under the heavy exactions of Angkorian rule, the impersonality and arbitrariness of Angkorian law, and the rigid hierarchy of Angkorian society, all of which were directly opposed by the simpler and more personalized qualities of their own society.

3

SUKHOTHAI
The Dawn of Happiness
1238–1378

Traditionally, the Thais date the birth of their nation to 1238 and the founding of Sukhothai, meaning in a phonetic form of Pali 'Dawn of Happiness', and they have come to regard the kingdom in semi-mythical fashion as a golden age. Sukhothai is unmistakably of great historical importance. It is equally certain that the 13th century was a Tai century; Khmer authority in the region was on the decline, while the numerical strength of Tai-speaking people migrating into the region was increasing dramatically.

However, it is misleading to think of a sudden and single burst of sunrise; there was a long and uneven build-up to the emergence of Tai supremacy in the territory now defined by national borders. Moreover, there were both prior and parallel developments, and the rise to power of Sukhothai, located on the northern edge of the Central Plains close by the Yom River, was contemporary with other nascent Tai states, particularly the consolidation of the northern Tai Lanna kingdom that was ultimately centred on Chiang Mai.

There is nonetheless a unique importance attached to Sukhothai, both in historical fact and in the popular consciousness of all Thais. As a sovereign state it was short-lived, but the political, religious, artistic and architectural patterns it established left an indelible stamp on the development of the nation that has never diminished.

THE BEGINNINGS

Early in the 13th century Sukhothai and nearby satellite settlements, notably Chalieng and Si Satchanalai, were part of the Khmer Empire, with the former assumed to be the administrative centre of the northern limits of Khmer control. This is supported by the evidence of the ruins of monuments that remain today, among the most prominent of which is Wat Si Sawai, preserved at what is now Sukhothai Historical Park, a World Heritage Site. Dating from the late 12th or early 13th century, the restored temple has three central Khmer-style towers (*prang*) and was most probably originally a shrine to the Hindu god Siva before being converted to Theravada Buddhist use. Similarly, the extensive ruins of Wat Phra Phai Luang show three separate stages of construction, and this structure was almost certainly first built as a Khmer Mahayana Buddhist temple.

While the Khmer held sway in the region, either by the direct rule of a governor or vassalage over petty states, groups of Tais were establishing increasingly powerful principalities. Evidence of the exact course of events is sketchy, and it can only be conjectured from ancient chronicles that Tai chieftains gradually increased their power through intermarriages with existing local ruling houses, be they Mon, Khmer or both.

Also, the Khmer did at times recognize some Tai rulers, awarding them official positions as viceroys in order to secure their loyalty to Angkor. One Tai chieftain to receive such recognition was Khun Pha Mueang, who ruled over a small principality named Mueang Rat, which was probably located somewhere near the present-day town of Uttaradit and was given the title Sri Indraditya. Khmer hopes that this would secure allegiance were misplaced, and according to traditional belief Tai *mueangs* grew more and more reluctant to pay tribute to the Khmer. It was then, in 1238 according to popular belief, but more likely in the early 1240s, that Khun Pha Mueang joined forces with Khun Bang Klang Hao, ruler of Mueang Bang Yang, and defeated the Khmer at Sukhothai.

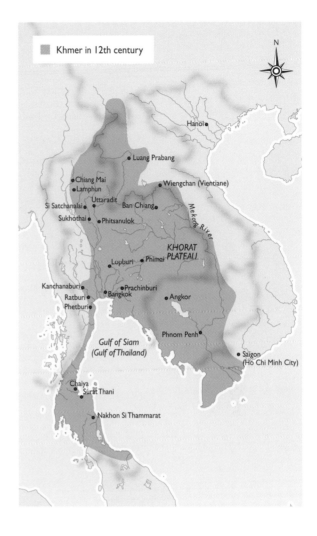

Whether because of his previous oath of allegiance to the Khmer or as a matter of seniority between the two Tai chieftains, Khun Pha Mueang ceded the victory along with his title to Khun Bang Klang Hao, who was duly crowned Si Indraditya, King of Sukhothai. The event made a profound impression on the local Tais, who honoured Si Indraditya's heroism with the title Phra Ruang, 'Glorious Prince', which was taken as the name of the Sukhothai dynasty, recognized by scholars as the first historical Thai dynasty.

It is not known how long Si Indraditya reigned, nor is there much evidence about the events of that reign. It would seem that the Khmer did not attempt to retake Sukhothai, largely because massive building programmes and wars against the kingdom of Champa would have depleted Angkor's resources, while the Khmer monarch at the time, King Jayavarman VIII (1243–1295), was by all accounts weak in his dealings with the Tai. Moreover, Tai strength in the region was being significantly boosted by waves of immigrants from Nanchao, in Yunnan, following its conquest in 1253 by the Mongols under Kublai Khan.

The main challenges to the new kingdom's authority came not from the Khmer but from neighbouring Tai principalities. In one incident the Prince of Sot, near present-day Mae Sot, attacked the western boundaries of Sukhothai. Initially Sri Indraditya's troops retreated and would have lost the day had it not been for the courage of the younger of the king's two sons, the 19-year-old Rama, who charged ahead on elephant back, engaged the attacking commander in one-on-one combat and defeated him, so earning the title Ramkhamhaeng, 'Rama the Bold'.

During the reign of Si Indraditya and that of his successor, his elder son Ban Mueang (dates unknown though approximated at 1270–1279), the territory ruled by Sukhothai was relatively small, probably extending no further west than Tak, north to Uttaradit, east to Phitsanulok and south to Kamphaeng Phet, all less than 100 kilometres (62 miles) from the capital. At this time the kingdom comprised the capital city and associated towns, those close to Sukhothai being ruled directly by officials appointed by the king, while settlements further away from the influence of the royal court were held together in a kind of feudal system. It was not until Ramkhamhaeng ascended the throne, probably in the late 1270s, that the kingdom was significantly expanded and consolidated politically, administratively, religiously and culturally.

KING RAMKHAMHAENG

The first Thai monarch to be accorded the title 'the Great' in the modern age, King Ramkhamhaeng was widely respected as a warrior. This factor, along with his assumed connections either by birth or by marriage with the ruling elite of other Tai states, augmented his authority, allowing him to exercise his personal qualities and fulfill considerable ambitions. He is credited with the creation of the Thai alphabet (adapted from a Khmer script, which was derived from the Indian Devanagari script), and with the adoption of Theravada Buddhism as the state religion. He further established a paternalistic style of rule that was in marked contrast to the Khmer concept of a god-king that had previously been dominant in the region.

Much of the information regarding Ramkhamhaeng's reign comes from a stone inscription reputedly discovered at Sukhothai's Wat Mahathat in 1833 by the future King Mongkut, at the time a monk and scholar before he succeeded to the throne in Bangkok as King Rama IV. The inscription describes, in what are generally accepted as Ramkhamhaeng's own words, an idealized state ruled over by a benign, almost fatherly lord. The text in part reads:

> In the time of King Ramkhamhaeng this land of Sukhothai is thriving. There are fish in the water and rice in the fields. The lord of the realm does not levy toll on his subjects for travelling the roads; . . . When commoners or men of rank differ and disagree [the King] examines the case to get at the truth and then settles it justly for them . . . He [the King] has hung a bell in the opening of the gate over there: if any commoner in the land has a grievance which sickens his belly and gripes his heart, and which he wants to make known to his ruler and lord, it is easy; he goes and strikes the bell which the King has hung there; King Ramkhamhaeng, the ruler of the kingdom, hears the call; he goes and questions the man, examines the case, and decides it justly for him.

Such vainglory can be read merely as Ramkhamhaeng's way of publicly rejecting the authoritarianism of Angkor to which the Tais had been subjected. Be that as it may, the authenticity of the stone inscription has been questioned in recent years; the argument, based on textual analysis, is that it was fabricated in the 19th century in order to add greater substance and legitimacy to the nation's early independence at a time when Western imperialism threatened. Most scholars, however, reject this argument and continue to accept the inscription as genuine, and while it tends to hyperbole, the truth of Sukhothai being well governed and prosperous is generally accepted.

Whatever the degree of Ramkhamhaeng's paternalism, he was an absolute ruler. (Some historians dispute the term 'absolute', arguing that until the late-19th century Thai kings were dependent to varying degrees on complex networks of personal

BELOW
Accredited to King Ramkamhaeng, this stone inscription discovered at Sukhothai in the 19th century gives a detailed account of an idealized state, a bountiful and prosperous realm ruled by a paternalistic lord.

OPPOSITE

Wat Chang Lom at Si Satchanalai, Sukhothai's second city, is a masterful architectural work that combines Sri Lankan and Mon influences and is distinguished by a fine bell-shaped chedi *with sculpted elephants* (chang) *surrounding the base.*

allegiances and alliances. For present purposes, however, 'absolute' is used as the opposite of 'constitutional'.) As head of the army he organized the government of his kingdom along military lines, with provincial governors and other officers holding military rank and serving under him. This does not mean that he expanded his territories solely or even largely through conquest. Ramkhamhaeng's political skills were as great as his military prowess; much of his kingdom was held together by a complex string of personal ties whereby a distant city's loyalty was derived indirectly through a chain of allegiances between different princes or governors in what was in effect a pyramid of power.

The strength of Sukhothai lay in the capital itself (Si Satchanalai, some 70 kilometres/44 miles to the north, was a second capital and the seat of the deputy king) and in the personal qualities of the king. Direct rule would have been limited largely to the capital and would have diminished in proportion to distance from it, provincial governors having considerable individual authority in their own areas. Although the kingdom lacked distinct borders, its sphere of influence under Ramkhamhaeng was considerable, encompassing Tak, Kamphaeng Phet, Phitsanulok, Phichit, Suphanburi, Ratburi, Phetburi and Nakhon Si Thammarat, as well as parts of lower Burma, eastern Laos and the Malay peninsula. Ramkhamhaeng further maintained friendly relations with the Tai rulers of the Lanna and Phayao kingdoms to the north, and also opened direct political relations with the Yuan Dynasty in China, to which he sent a number of embassies, the first in 1292.

RAMKHAMHAENG AND THERAVADA BUDDHISM

As important as Sukhothai's political and territorial gains was its consolidation of Theravada Buddhism as the national religion, making it a true Buddhist state. The Tai had already begun to adopt Theravada Buddhism in the 12th century. Groups of monks, Mon and Khmer as well as Tai, had travelled to study in Sri Lanka, the bastion of the faith, but it was Ramkhamhaeng who established it in Sukhothai. While on a tour of his territories he came into contact with the 'purified' teachings of Theravada Buddhism at the southern city of Nakhon Si Thammarat, and invited monks of the Lankan school to his capital. Their influence was later strengthened when missions made direct contact with Sri Lanka. The population embraced the faith, as witnessed today in the ruins of numerous temples that were built in Sukhothai and cities throughout the kingdom, which supported a large monastic community. Moreover Ramkhamhaeng is supposed to have given his public throne, on which he heard and settled claims from plaintiffs, over to Theravada Buddhist monks to deliver weekly sermons.

The impact of religion, art and architecture at this time cannot be underestimated, both politically and culturally. The religion was political in that it provided a foundation for political unity and identity, while the art and architecture inspired by the Lankan school established forms and a style that characterized not only the culture of Sukhothai, but have also endured throughout later periods in the evolution of a national art. Of the Sri Lankan architectural influences, the most readily seen is the bell-shaped *chedi*, a reliquary tower that forms an integral part of Thai temple architecture. The body of this style of tower is shaped like a large bell built on a square or octagonal base with diminishing tiers and topped by a tall, graceful spire. Imposing examples of the style can be seen today at Wat Chana Songkhram in Sukhothai, dating most probably from the 14th century, and at the late 14th-century Wat Chang Lom in Si Satchanalai (see page 49).

THE DECLINE OF SUKHOTHAI

For a kingdom with its power dependent on the strength of character and personal attributes of its ruler, it is not surprising that Sukhothai was weakened and lost territory after the death of Ramkhamhaeng in 1298. None of the six monarchs who followed rivalled Ramkhamhaeng in terms of political acumen, diplomacy or military prowess. Under Ramkhamhaeng's son and successor King Loe Thai (1298–1346/7) disintegration was rapid. Control over Uttaradit was lost at the start of the reign and in 1321 Tak, one of the oldest of Sukhothai's domains, was taken by Lanna, while access southwards was impeded by the loss of Suphanburi.

Political and territorial decline did not inhibit advancements in art and architecture, which continued to develop and would remain as the kingdom's most lasting legacy. One notable result of Ramkhamhaeng's trade missions to China was a stimulus to the production and widespread export of superb Chinese-style *Sawankhalok* ceramics. Moreover religious architecture, along with Buddhist sculpture, created a new aesthetic that reached an unprecedented pinnacle during the reign of King Lue Thai (Mahathammaracha I, 1347–1368/74?), Ramkhamhaeng's grandson. The 'lotus bud' *chedi*, for example, in which the spire is given

a graceful bud-like form, was a Sukhothai innovation, although perhaps nothing so distinguishes the period as images of the Buddha, most famously those of the Walking Buddha. The fluid, flowing lines and highly stylized physiognomy of these statues are extraordinary, and they have arguably never been surpassed by subsequent schools of Thai art.

SUKHOTHAI SCULPTURE

Buddha images of the Sukhothai period were far more stylized than anything that had gone before. Highlighting the Buddha's supernatural physical features, such as a cranial protuberance and extended ear lobes that follow descriptions of the Enlightened One in the Sri Lankan Pali texts, Sukhothai sculpture is marked by a greater fluidity in the line of the body and an uncanny degree of serenity and spirituality expressed in the facial features. Statues in the seated posture were popular, but the real triumph of the Sukhothai artists was the Walking Buddha. This posture had only appeared before in carved relief and it was a Thai innovation to produce walking images in the round. Not only was originality achieved, but it was also achieved in a most stunning fashion, with the artists brilliantly capturing their subject in a frozen moment of movement.

In other spheres, King Lue Thai is credited as the author of the *Trai Phum Phra Ruang* ('The Three Worlds According to King Ruang'), an important moral treatise on the Three Worlds (Heaven, Earth and Hell) in Buddhist cosmology. According to legend, this devout and scholarly monarch consulted more than 30 ancient texts to produce a work that is generally taken as the second oldest Thai book, if one accepts Ramkhamhaeng's stone inscriptions as the first. Handed down in various later versions, the *Trai Phum Phra Ruang* is considered a significant study on the essence of Buddhism that has shaped Thai thinking in diverse ways, as well as influencing traditional painting, sculpture, literature and architecture.

Lue Thai is also noted as the builder of several major religious monuments, including Wat Traphang Thong at Sukhothai and Wat Chedi Chet Thaew at Si Satchanalai, as well as for the creation of an administrative centre at Kamphaeng Phet, about 80 kilometres (50 miles) south of Sukhothai on the banks of the Ping River. The name translates as 'Diamond Wall', and the town was an important line of defence for Sukhothai; after the latter's demise it continued to be a strategic base between Ayutthaya and the northern Lanna kingdom. Less well preserved today than Sukhothai or Si Satchanalai, Kamphaeng Phet nonetheless displays significant ruins attesting to the period's architectural achievements.

Lue Thai was succeeded by King Mahathammaracha II (1368/74?–1398). Sukhothai, now reduced to a local rather than a regional force and weakened in manpower by frequent wars with neighbouring states, finally became a vassal state of the younger Thai Kingdom of Ayutthaya when, in 1378, Mahathammaracha II surrendered the city in the face of superior forces. Thus ended 140 years of independence. The Phra Ruang dynasty continued until the death of King Mahathammaracha IV in 1438, after which Ayutthaya appointed its own royal governor to rule over its northern territories, with his seat of office at Phitsanulok, thus absorbing Sukhothai as a province of the Kingdom of Ayutthaya. Eventually, in the 16th century, Sukhothai was abandoned, as was Si Satchanalai. Of the first Thai kingdom's three principal sites only Kamphaeng Phet survived as a living settlement.

ABOVE
Kamphaeng Phet, the third of Sukhothai's three major cities, displays the ruins of a number of architectural monuments, although it is most noted today for its many and varied Buddha sculptures that well illustrate Sukhothai style.

4

CHIANG MAI
The Kingdom of Lanna
1296–1558

Chiang Mai was founded in 1296 by King Mengrai as the capital of his Lanna Thai kingdom; two and a half centuries later the state lost its independence to the Burmese. These are important milestones in Thailand's sovereign history, but Lanna long predates Chiang Mai, while northern Thailand, with mixed fortunes, maintained a degree of autonomy until the early 20th century, and Chiang Mai today remains the nation's second city. Hence the dates are used here merely for convenience, as historical markers that need some introduction and a postscript to round out the picture.

BEFORE LANNA

The period before the founding of the Lanna kingdom is problematic for its lack of sure evidence regarding embryonic Tai states. This is especially the case with what is known as Yonok Country, reputedly centred on Chiang Saen by the banks of the Mekong River in northern Thailand.

According to one early Tai chronicle, in around the 7th century a Tai chief from Sipsongpanna, in southern Yunnan, moved into the area of Chiang Saen with a large band of followers. He imposed his authority over the local hill peoples, creating a sizeable kingdom that extended north to Yunnan, bordered Vietnam to the east and the Shan region of Myanmar to the west, and possibly reached as far south as Lopburi. Other accounts, however, record that local Khmer rulers resisted and that Yonok Country was invaded by the Angkor Empire. While various versions of the early chronicles relate tales of Yonok Country from the mid-7th to the 11th century, they are so fragmentary and contradictory that it is impossible to say how true they are without any archaeological evidence. Nonetheless, the fact that they exist does indicate the possibility of an expansionist Tai state around Chiang Saen well before the 13th century.

OPPOSITE
The original city of Chiang Mai was meticulously planned by King Mengrai and it still forms the heart of the modern, much expanded metropolis, though most of the walls and other fortifications seen today are reconstructions.

There are good reasons why Chiang Saen should have arisen as a strategic centre. The Mekong River provides a natural defensive barrier to the east, while other nearby rivers, the Mae Kok, Mae Chan and Mae Ruak, would have well served transportation and communication needs. Archaeological evidence today reveals fortification walls and the remains of more than 120 monuments in and around the modern town. These date mostly to the 14th century, but it is generally accepted that they were built over earlier constructions. For example, some archaeologists argue that Wat Chedi Luang could originally have been built in the 12th century, and Wat Pa Sak, still an imposing monument today, possibly dates back to the late 13th century. Given the widespread practice of raising new monuments over pre-existing structures, what survives at Chiang Saen suggests that it was both an early and a significant power base.

Regardless of doubts pertaining to the early legends of Yonok Country, it survived into the beginning of the 11th century, when Buddhism spread through the area, probably brought via trade links with Haripunchai and beyond to other Mon cities in what is now coastal Myanmar. David K. Wyatt writes that:

> This was a development of immense cultural significance, for it transformed a weak and localized folk Buddhism . . . into a universal, institutionalized religious tradition, linked with the Theravada Buddhist civilizations of the Mons and Ceylon [Sri Lanka]. It integrated the Tai into a wider 'community of the faithful', in which the Tai could feel they belonged. It supplanted local animistic spirits with more universal values and encouraged an ethic with social dimensions that trancended the village and *mueang*.

The spread of Buddhism to northern Thailand was thus parallelled by social changes, not only through the assimilation of indigenous cultures, but also by the Tai's increasing movement into lowland areas. Here land availability and irrigation allowed for the development of wet-rice cultivation that could support larger settlements than before, as well as freeing a proportion of the population from agricultural work and so fostering the growth of military and ruling classes. It was still a time of feudalism and warfare (involving raiding parties more than protracted aggression), but by the end of the 12th century Tai *mueang* were poised to exert domination over their neighbours.

Traditional ritual bathing of the statue of King Mengrai in Chiang Rai town during the annual Songkran (Thai New Year) festival.

THE BEGINNING OF LANNA: 1239–1317

Chiang Saen emerges from the legends of Yonok Country as the birthplace of Mengrai in 1239. He rose to power to become the first monarch of the kingdom of Lanna (the name translates as 'Land of a Million Rice Fields'), which eventually controlled most of what is now northern Thailand.

In the early 13th century a number of Tai principalities were scattered throughout the Mekong River area of northern Thailand and southern Yunnan. Mengrai's father ruled Chiang Saen, while his mother was the daughter of the ruler of the Lue state of Chiang Hung, and Mengrai considered himself to be the descendant of a true royal line with legitimacy to rule the region. When he succeeded his father in 1259 he showed determination to bring neighbouring Tai *mueang*, which were often at war with each other, under his unifying authority.

Popularly credited with the attributes of wisdom, benevolence and foresight, Mengrai was certainly an ambitious conqueror. In quick succession he expanded his control over the principalities of Mueang Lai, Chiang Kham and Chiang Chang, where he appointed his own officers to administer them. Next he turned south and in 1262 founded a new city on the banks of the Kok River, Chiang Rai, which he named after himself. Although the city was later eclipsed as Lanna's capital and today displays little of its ancient history, it long retained importance as a trading centre. It is also here that Mengrai's ashes are enshrined in the *chedi* of Wat Ngam Mueang, originally built in 1318, although the structure seen today is of a much later date (see page 61).

Using Chiang Rai as a power base, Mengrai went on to extend his authority over Chiang Khong, on the Mekong to the north-east and Fang to the west; then, in 1274, he looked to conquer the Mon kingdom of Haripunchai (Lamphun). The city had long been established as a Mon stronghold dating back to the 8th century. An idea of its sophistication can be gained today at Lamphun's Wat Ku Kut (Wat Chamathewi), where there are two beautiful brick *chedis* decorated with stucco figures of the Buddha dating from the early 13th century. Among the last surviving examples of Dvaravati architecture, the larger of the two is in the form of a stepped pyramid 21 metres (69 feet) high, while the smaller *chedi* is built on an octagonal plan.

Defended by moats and ramparts, Haripunchai was a far tougher proposition than the Tai *mueang* that Mengrai had so far subdued. Realizing that he could not take it by force he decided instead on guile, sending Ai Fa, a Mon officer in his retinue, to seek employment at the royal court and work secretly to sow dissent among the people and undermine the authority of the king, and so soften the kingdom for capture. It would take seven years before this plan reached fruition.

In the meantime Mengrai sought to expand his territory south-east and in 1276 led his army to Phayao, but the local king, Ngam Mueang, extended friendship and managed to secure an alliance with Mengrai (Phayao was later annexed by Lanna after the death of Ngam Mueang). This set something of a pattern of amity among local Tai rulers. A few years later Mengrai was asked to settle a dispute between Ngam Mueang and King Ramkhamhaeng of Sukhothai (according to legend Ramkhamhaeng had seduced Ngam Mueang's wife). He acted the diplomat and brought about a reconciliation that resulted in the three rulers swearing a pact of friendship.

Doubtless mutual benefit lay behind such cordiality – Mongol advances into Myanmar at the time posed a common threat to the three rulers – but what is most historically significant about the pact is its implicit recognition of common ties and relationships, in short a shared Tai identity.

Shortly after this harmonious interlude, Mengrai learned that Ai Fa had succeeded in fermenting popular discontent with King Yi Ba of Haripunchai, thus paving the way for a successor. In 1281 Mengrai arrived in Haripunchai at the head of a large army. The confusion sown by Ai Fa amongst the population made force scarcely necessary, and Mengrai had little difficulty in taking Haripunchai and ascending the throne. This made him the paramount power in the entire northern region, stretching east–west from what is today Laos to the Shan States in Myanmar. The gain was not just political, but also cultural. Haripunchai had been the foremost civilization in the region, a religious and artistic centre, and its legacy enhanced the supremacy of the Lanna kingdom.

As much as he was a conqueror pursuing an expansionist policy, Mengrai was no simple militarist and appears to have avoided hostility between Tai states and their immediate neighbours as far as possible. Cases in point are the fact that he allowed the defeated King Yi Ba of Haripunchai to live in Lampang, a short distance to the south-east (until he fled after staging an unsuccessful rebellion in 1296); and the alliance he forged with the King of Pegu, the Mon capital in lower Myanmar, in the late 1280s (a pact that was reputedly sealed by Mengrai accepting the king's daughter in marriage).

Mengrai further respected Mon culture and Theravada Buddhism, of which he became a patron. This, together with political alliances and the recognition of royal lineage, came in time to define Lanna and its people not as Mon or Tai, but as *Tai Yuan*, 'Northern Thai'.

In spite of Haripunchai having been taken intact, Mengrai chose not to reside there and moved his capital several times over the next few years. Finally, in 1292, he decided on a location by the banks of the Ping River some 25 kilometres (15 miles) north of Haripunchai. Initially he favoured the river's east bank and settled at Wiang Kum Kam, which had originally been built by the Mon in the 11th or 12th century as a fortified satellite town of Haripunchai. He carried

OPPOSITE
Paying respects at the memorial to King Mengrai in the compound of Wat Ngam Mueang, Chiang Rai, where the chedi enshrines the ashes of the city's founder.

out a considerable building programme here and archaeological excavations have revealed several ruined temples, including Wat Chedi Si Liam, built in the Mon style with a stepped pyramid form and thought to have been modelled on Wat Ku Kut in Lamphun.

For unknown reasons Mengrai became dissatisfied with the site of Wiang Kum Kam and decided to build a much larger city on the opposite bank of the Ping River. He took extraordinary care over the planning of this city, named Chiang Mai ('New City'), and reputedly consulted his allies, King Ngam Mueang of Phayao and Sukhothai's King Ramkhamhaeng, over its design and fortification; the construction began in 1296.

Walled and moated and built on a grand layout, Chiang Mai marks the consolidation of the kingdom Mengrai had carved out for himself and named Lanna, the territory of which came to encompass present-day northern Thailand; Chiang Mai itself developed as the region's major political, commercial and cultural focal point.

The Thai chronicles record that – as befitting a legendary ruler – Mengrai died in dramatic fashion after being struck by a bolt of lightning in 1317. The period immediately following his death was not auspicious. Dynastic squabbles led to there being four kings (one reigning twice) in 11 years. Only in 1328 did King Kham Fu, Mengrai's great-grandson, start to bring a steadying hand to the state. However, Mengrai had over more than half a century established a well-organized kingdom with a definable national identity and a dynasty that would rule over northern Thailand for the next two centuries. It is important to note, however, that Lanna, like other early Tai kingdoms, was not a nation-state as the term is understood today, but rather a network of alliances in a pattern of dominance and submission, the degree of which depended largely on the strength and ability of individual Lanna kings.

THE GOLDEN AGE: 1355–c. 1526

The ancient chronicles of Lanna are filled with wars, battles and sieges in a near-endless saga of conflict with virtually all of its neighbours at one time or another, and often today's ally would become tomorrow's foe. As if wars with other polities were not enough, Lanna was frequently at war with itself in tussles for the throne; the greatest asset of kingship was not statesmanship, but military prowess backed by Byzantine skills of intrigue. Strangely, none of this prevented the kingdom from attaining its greatest geographical extent, as well as refining a high culture in which Theravada Buddhism and the arts flourished and left a legacy that still distinguishes northern Thailand as in many ways a land apart.

That Lanna experienced a golden age in the 15th century in spite of the conflicts was partly due to the personal nature of antagonisms, especially among the leadership (leaving most of the population unaffected). It was personal relationships that accounted for prosperity; the produce and manpower of numerous semi-autonomous principalities were commanded by the kings of Chiang Mai through local government put in the hands of brothers, sons and trusted associates.

OPPOSITE
Temple ruins and other monuments remain to mark the site of Wiang Kum Kam, originally a Mon city where King Mengrai based himself immediately prior to his founding of Chiang Mai as the new capital of Lanna.

OVERLEAF
The Rai Mae Fah Luang Art and Cultural Park in Chiang Rai showcases traditional Lanna architecture and crafts that characterize a distinctive northern Thai style.

Following a somewhat restless period after the death of King Mengrai, King Ku Na (1355–1385) laid the foundations for Lanna's cultural blossoming. Both politically adept and highly educated in the arts and sciences, he invited the Venerable Sumana, a Sukhothai monk, to settle in the kingdom and establish a Sri Lankan sect of forest-dwelling Buddhist monks. In its enduring work, from the production of written texts to the founding of monasteries, the sect, supported by royal patronage, was to have a lasting religious, intellectual and cultural impact that served to reinforce Lanna's statehood and identity.

While Chiang Mai became a religious and cultural hub, internal and external politics continued in a litany of hostilities between kings and usurpers, and battles with Ayutthaya, the younger Thai kingdom to the south, and – most immediately threateningly – Yunnan, which launched an unsuccessful attack on Chiang Saen in 1404. The two reigns following the death of Ku Na in 1385, that of King Saen Mueang Ma (1385–1401) and King Sam Fang Kaen (1401–1441),

LEFT AND OPPOSITE
*Background details in
otherwise religious temple
mural paintings frequently
include scenes, often
humorous, of daily life.
Pictured here at Wat Phumin,
in the northern city of Nan,
are, respectively, a particularly
charming portrait of a courting
couple, the man's tattoos and
the woman earrings, as well as
the hairstyles of both, being of
special note, and a formation
of soldiers.*

were typically muddied by court intrigue, as was the succession of King Tilokaracha (1441–1487), who as the sixth son of Sam Fang Kaen came to the throne
only after a palace coup. This nonetheless had a fortuitous outcome as Tilokaracha is now regarded as Lanna's greatest monarch, with his reign representing the
kingdom's zenith.

Tilokaracha was initially preoccupied with securing his authority, as well as
with defending Lamphun from an attack by Ayutthaya and being forced into a
war with Nan, a power centre in the east of the region, which resulted in 1449
with the latter submitting to Lanna rule. Later in his reign there would be other
wars with the Shan to the west and, in the east, with the Vietnamese, who threatened Nan after having invaded Luang Prabang (in what is today Laos). However,
the war that dominates the history of the period was with Ayutthaya.

WAR WITH AYUTTHAYA

On-off hostilities between Chiang Mai and Ayutthaya lasted nearly 30 years, beginning in the mid-1450s with an attack by Ayutthaya on Phrae and Lampang. Subsequent action, played out mainly around Kamphaeng Phet and Phitsanulok (where Ayutthaya's King Trailok had set up a temporary capital in order to better oversee operations), was inconclusive, with neither side being able to gain any sustainable advantage. During interludes in the fighting war was waged through spies, with King Trailok planting a sorcerer-monk in Chiang Mai and King Tilokaracha sending spies into Phitsanulok and Ayutthaya. These appear to have been more effective than one might imagine, and, as David K. Wyatt records, Trailok's sorcerer-monk succeeded in causing considerable damage, not least in having Tilokaracha's only son and heir falsely accused of plotting a rebellion and executed. Later, the spy himself was exposed and beaten to death.

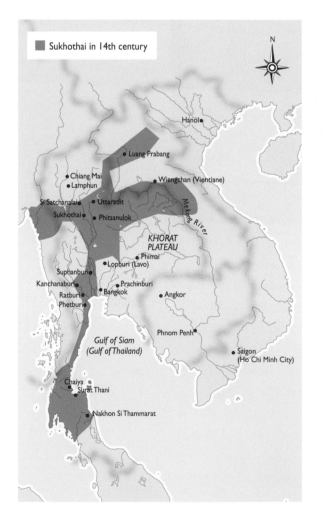

In spite of near-incessant warring with one party or another and the unresolved struggle against Ayutthaya, Lanna at this time was at its strongest and most respected, recognized as a regional power able to treat on equal terms with both the Burmese and the Thais of Ayutthaya. It had also reached its greatest territorial extent, commanding the area east to west from the Mekong River to the Salween, and from Chiang Rung in the north down to Sukhothai in the south. It is worth noting that warfare of the period had a cultural effect in that captured communities, especially those including artisans, were transplanted in the victor's territories. These movements of peope boosted populations and the development of skilled craftsmanship, as well as providing the manpower to increase agricultural production and ensure a surplus.

The latter years of Tilokaracha's reign were marked by activities that underscored Lanna's religious and cultural importance. A literally towering achievement was the *chedi* at Wat Chedi Luang in Chiang Mai, which Tilokaracha had constructed to a height of 96 metres (315 feet) between 1475 and 1478. Although it was partially destroyed by an earthquake in 1545, it remained the tallest structure in the city until the 1950s. Chiang Mai's standing in the Buddhist world was also enhanced when Tilokaracha sponsored the Eighth Buddhist World Council in 1477, which was held, as generally believed, at Wat Chet Yot. According to the chronicles, this temple (which is still standing) was specially commissioned by the Lanna king. It is unique among northern Thai religious architecture, with its seven *chedis* raised on a rectangular base and copied either directly from the Mahabodhi Temple at Bodhgaya, India, or from replicas seen in Myanmar.

After Tilokaracha, Lanna was again subjected to the old-style princely struggles. King Yot Chiang Rai (1487–1495), Tilokaracha's grandson, so dissatisfied his ministers that he was deposed and replaced by his 13-year-old son, King Mueang Kaeo (1495–1526). This was the last Lanna reign of any real strength; Mueang Kaeo was in many ways a determined monarch, both politically and in his devotion to the Buddhist faith. However, his military ambitions met with crushing defeats; in particular Lampang fell to Ayutthaya in 1515 and a major expedition against the Shan state of Keng Tung in 1523 failed miserably.

Lanna's dominance was now greatly reduced and the kingdom was further weakened by dynastic struggles that were even more violent and bloody than those that had been before and culminated in four years of virtual civil war in the mid-16th century. Adding to Chiang Mai's woes was the devastating earthquake of 1545. Unable to recover from the chaos, Lanna fell victim to the expansion drive of the Burmese King Bayinnaung of Pegu and surrendered to his invading forces in 1558.

ABOVE

A reconstructed naga (dragon-headed mythical serpent) guards the approach to Wat Chedi Luang, Chiang Mai.

OPPOSITE

The extent of the Sukhothai and Lanna kingdoms in the 14th century. Not all of the area would have been under direct control and the power of kings depended largely on allegiances and alliances with the local rulers of the more distant regions.

DECLINE AND RESURGENCE

Lanna was to remain under the sway of the Burmese, with intermittent spells of self-government for the next two centuries. However, there was no direct occupation, or any form of colonization. Bayinnaung initially made Wisutthithewi – a member of the Lanna royal family – queen, and on her death in 1578 appointed one of his sons to rule as viceroy. Judging by the chronicles, the northern Thai at first bore little resentment against the Burmese and seemed willingly to have accepted suzerainty and the payment of an annual tribute. As far as the general population was concerned life went on very much as before.

With a succession of puppet rulers, Chiang Mai lost effective authority over the north and Lanna was reduced to numerous small *mueang* that were more or less self-ruling and extremely wary of each other. Occasional rebellions by various Lanna factions against their Burmese overlords all failed, and the region was increasingly caught up in the ongoing conflict between the Thai Kingdom of Ayutthaya to the south and Burma to the west. Antagonism between the two was protracted and inconclusive as fortunes fluctuated, and although Ayutthaya forces did at various times manage to invade and occupy Burmese Lanna the gains were always short-lived.

Finally, in 1767, the Burmese succeeded in destroying Ayutthaya, one of the repercussions of which was Burma's greatly intensified oppression of Lanna. This included the forced conscription of a northern Thai army to aid in a Burmese attack on Luang Prabang (Laos), which, along with the general upheaval that saw villages and crops destroyed, both drained Lanna of manpower and reduced it to poverty.

Out of the chaos emerged two key figures – Phraya Taksin, a Thai general, and Chao Kavila, the ruler of the Lanna town of Lampang. Taksin swiftly rallied the Thais after the fall of Ayutthaya and founded a new Thai kingdom centred on Thonburi in late 1769. In the north, Kavila rebelled against the Burmese and in 1774 succeeded in retaking Chiang Mai, which he formally handed over to the Thai army under Taksin, who appointed him as governor. However, Chiang Mai was so devastated and depopulated that it was abandoned, and Kavila returned to Lampang.

Fierce fighting against the Burmese, who retained strongholds at Chiang Rai and Chiang Saen, continued for several years. Not until around 1800 was Kavila

The Burmese style mondop at Wat Phra Kaeo Don Tao, one of Lampang's oldest and most venerable temples, was added in 1909 and illustrates an enduring Burmese influence on Lanna art and architecture and, indeed, on the culture of the region as a whole.

able to return to Chiang Mai and set about rebuilding the city and re-establishing it as the capital of Lanna. By now the Chakri dynasty had been founded at the new Thai capital of Bangkok, to which Kavila swore allegiance; in turn he was confirmed as the governor (*chao*) of Chiang Mai.

In 1804 the Burmese were ultimately defeated at Chiang Saen. Kavila, with his brothers ruling in Lampang and Lamphun, gradually brought the smaller *mueangs* of the north back into the Lanna fold, which by the time of his death in 1813 had been resurrected to something close to the Lanna kingdom of old.

Although ostensibly under the control of the Bangkok government, Chiang Mai was neglected and left pretty much to itself. It was not until the late 19th century, when British colonial interests in neighbouring Burma were seen as a potential threat, that a high commissioner was appointed to bring the area under the direct authority of Bangkok. Even then, quasi autonomy remained until the death of the last *chao* of Chiang Mai in 1939.

Throughout the first half of the 20th century, telegraph, railway and other modern developments increasingly involved Chiang Mai in the political and social spheres of the Thai nation state, into which it and the other regions of the north were fully engaged as provinces. However, while assimilating Thai customs and language, northern Thailand was enriched by the Burmese, whose art and architecture, culinary styles and other influences were absorbed and became a lasting dimension of Lanna identity.

5

AYUTTHAYA
The Power and the Glory
1351–1767

Sukhothai briefly and Lanna more enduringly can be termed 'kingdoms' in that they variously absorbed, united or extended authority over smaller Tai states that had arisen throughout the region by the mid-14th century, and in so doing made considerable political and cultural advances. Yet neither had a true international outlook, or rivalled the administrative sophistication of the Angkor Empire. It was the rise of Ayutthaya that would transform the Tai world and lead to the creation of a Thai nation that engaged with the outside world in politics and international trade relations.

THE RISE OF AYUTTHAYA
(1351–1488)

In the collapsing, post-Ramkhamhaeng Sukhothai world, the two Tai states that seemed to have remained strongest were Lopburi (Lavo), ostensibly in the sphere of the Khmer though doggedly holding itself independent of both Angkor and Sukhothai, and Suphanburi, which was predominantly Tai and Theravada Buddhist. Out of this environment in the mid-14th century appeared U Thong, 'an obscure adventurer', as David K. Wyatt describes him, who married a daughter of the ruler of Suphanburi and also possibly married into the ruling family of Lopburi. Subsequently he founded the kingdom of Ayutthaya.

RIGHT
*Still revered, a partially
ruined Buddha image in the
compound of Wat Phra Sri
Sanphet is adorned by a votive
flower garland.*

OPPOSITE
*A Buddha head entwined
by tree roots at Ayutthaya's
Wat Ratchaburana presents
a haunting image of the
passage of time.*

THE FOUNDING OF AYUTTHAYA

According to the Royal Chronicles of Ayutthaya, U Thong was chosen as the ruler of Lopburi by its people in the absence of any successor from the royal family in 1350 or 1351. At that time a smallpox (some sources say cholera) epidemic broke out, and U Thong moved the population out of Lopburi to the south for safety. He and his troops then marched for 'several days until they came to a large river and saw a circular island, smooth, level, and apparently clean, standing in the centre of the area'. U Thong decided to found a new capital on the spot, so Ayutthaya was established 'in 712, a Year of the Tiger, second of the decade, on Friday, the sixth day of the waxing moon of the fifth month', which translates as Friday, 4 March 1351.

An alternative version of Ayutthaya's founding holds that it was already a thriving city and trade centre and U Thong chose it as his capital because it was best positioned for him to control his expanding domains. Located at the confluence of the Chao Phraya, Lopburi and Pa Sak Rivers, Ayutthaya had the natural protection of an island city. It was also well placed for trade and communications as a port city, with the Chao Phraya providing access to the Gulf of Thailand some 80 kilometres (50 miles) downstream. In the 16th and 17th centuries the latter would serve as an international gateway for Western diplomatic and trade missions that put Ayutthaya on the world map.

RIGHT

A memorial statue of U Thong, later King Ramathibodi, commemorates the founder of Ayutthaya who rose from obscurity to be chosen as the monarch of a new Tai kingdom.

ABOVE

Wat Phu Khao Thong stands on the site of a Mon-style chedi erected by Burmese King Bayinnaung to commemorate his victory over Ayutthaya in 1569. After it fell into decay, it was rebuilt in Thai style by King Borommakot in 1745.

OPPOSITE

Map showing the territorial extent of, respectively, the Lanna and Ayutthaya kingdoms in the 15th century.

On his coronation U Thong took the name King Ramathibodi and quickly set about consolidating his power base, first securing the two strongest regional centres, Lopburi and Suphanburi, by appointing his son Ramesuan and his brother-in-law Borommaracha to govern each respectively. This was to be the pattern that defined the Kingdom of Ayutthaya less as a unified state and more as a mosaic of largely self-governing principalities and vassal states that owed allegiance to the king. The most important or powerful areas were usually under the control of members of the royal family, although others were ruled by local leaders with sufficient military might. The system succeeded through a strong monarchy, but was an internal weakness at times of royal succession when, with no law of succession, rivalries often arose. It should be noted that there was no real sense of nationhood at this time, any more than there was in Europe of the day, and the people were sworn followers of a king rather than citizens of a state.

Problems with succession arose after the death of Ramathibodi in 1369, with Ramesuan taking the throne in accordance with his father's wishes, only to surrender it shortly afterwards to his powerful uncle, Borommaracha. When Borommaracha I died in 1388 his teenage son, Thong Chan, reigned for just seven days before Ramesuan marched on Ayutthaya, had Thong Chan executed (clubbed to death in a velvet sack, as was the royal custom) and regained the throne. In its 416-year history, Ayutthaya was to have 33 kings and five dynasties.

If succession was a weak point, the institution of the monarchy itself was all powerful. During Ramathibodi's reign the paternalistic style of Sukhothai's King Ramkhamhaeng was abandoned in favour of absolute monarchy based on the concept of divine kingship, founded on both Hindu and Buddhist beliefs, while Theravada Buddhism remained the national religion. The king was an autocrat, all the land of the country belonging to him, and a special court language grew up to be used to communicate with or about royalty and royal possessions.

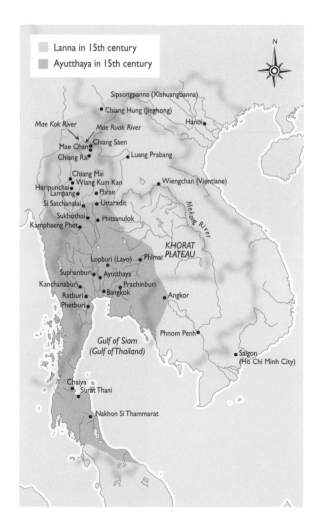

In spite of rivalries over succession and changes of dynasty, the institution of the monarchy was quintessential of the Ayutthaya era, and at the kingdom's height in the 17th century it was remarked on by virtually all European travellers. 'The king has absolute power. He is truly the god of the Siamese; no-one dares utter his name', wrote Abbé de Choisy, who accompanied a French mission to the court of Ayutthaya in 1685.

The system of administration was greatly strengthened by Ramathibodi, who created the offices of the four Great Officials – corresponding, respectively, to ministers for local government, the Royal Household, finance and agriculture. A legal code, the *Dharmashastra* (a compilation that included, among others, the Law of Evidence, the Law on Offences against the Government and the Law on Offences against the People), was compiled to assist these officers in the execution their duties. A bureaucracy based on a hierarchy of clearly ranked officials was thus effectively created. Society as a whole became similarly structured, as a pyramid with the king at the apex, and the interrelationship of merit, wealth, status and political influence determining a descending order.

In his 18-year reign Ramathibodi had laid a solid foundation on which his successors could build. In addition to administrative and political advances he had secured Ayutthaya's eastern frontier, with the army under Borommaracha decisively defeating the Khmer after an initial invasion of Cambodia led by Prince Ramesuan in 1352 had failed.

After wresting the throne from Ramesuan in 1370, Borommaracha, now King Borommaracha, turned his belligerent eye to the north and in 1372 attempted to invade the Kingdom of Sukhothai. He was initially thwarted, mainly by Lanna troops coming to the aid of their ally. Only after two other unsuccessful invasions was Sukhothai finally forced into submission, becoming a vassal of Ayutthaya in 1378 following the capture of Nakhon Sawan, Phitsanulok and Kamphaeng Phet.

LEFT
Dating from the 14th century and enshrined in Phitsanulok's Wat Phra Si Ratana Mahathat temple, the late Sukhothai-style Phra Phuttha Chinnarat remains one of Thailand's most revered Buddha images.

OPPOSITE
Ruins of an ancient temple are reminders of the importance of Phitsanulok during the Ayutthaya period, when it occupied a strategic position at the northern extent of the kingdom's territory.

Borommaracha's next target was Lanna, which had incurred his wrath for aiding Sukhothai. No long-term gains were made, however, and the old warrior king finally succumbed to illness in 1388 on his way home from a campaign against a rebellious Kamphaeng Phet.

According to the royal chronicles, Ramesuan's second reign of seven years (1388–1395) saw continued warfare with Lanna and Angkor, although victories credited to Ayutthaya are unverified. In the see-saw nature of Ayutthaya's conflict, King Ramaracha (1395–1409), Ramesuan's son, had to contend with a renewed fight-back by Sukhothai, which managed to take Nakhon Sawan in 1400. This was a severe loss to Ayutthaya as the location served as a vital river and communications junction.

Ramaracha was deposed and exiled in the course of some unexplained internal conflict and it was King Intharacha (1409–1424), a man aged more than 50 with considerable experience in government as regional ruler of Suphanburi, who reasserted Ayutthaya's authority over Sukhothai. The precise events of his reign are unrecorded, although it is believed that in 1419 he backed Mahathammaracha IV in a succession struggle for the Sukhothai throne.

On the death of King Intharacha there was a bizarre turn of events when his two elder sons vied for the throne and sought to settle the dispute by a duel

on elephant back, in the course of which both were thrown from their mounts and killed instantly. The event is recalled today by the ruins of Wat Ratchaburana, preserved in Ayutthaya Historical Park, which was built in 1424 on the cremation site of the two brothers by their younger sibling, who was crowned King Borommaracha II (1424–1448). Unexpected though the succession was, Borommaracha II proved himself to be a more than able monarch, consolidating earlier gains and positioning Ayutthaya to become the major power in mainland Southeast Asia.

By this time Angkor was well in decline, and Borommaracha II finally concluded Ayutthaya's years of struggle against the Khmer by taking and looting their capital in 1431–1432. A few years later Sukhothai was absorbed into the Kingdom of Ayutthaya on the death of its last monarch, Mahathammaracha IV, in 1438. With his eastern flank now secure and the northern frontier extended,

Borommaracha II next looked to Lanna and initiated warfare that would be more or less continuous for the next hundred years.

On his death in 1448, Borommaracha II's son Ramesuan took the title King Borommatrailokanat, usually shortened to Trailok (1448–1488), ruling over a kingdom that was larger, more powerful and more populous than ever before. Trailok would be largely engaged in pursing the war with Lanna, and yet, inheriting a huge kingdom, he saw the need for government reforms that would strengthen administrative institutions. Ayutthaya had been highly organized and tightly controlled from the beginning, and part of its strength lay in its ability to command manpower. Under Trailok new laws were introduced that more clearly defined a complex hierarchy. The position and responsibility of everyone was ranked and recognized, and rewarded through a system of land tenure known as *sakdi na*, translating literally as 'the power of rice fields'.

A NEW SYSTEM OF LAND TENURE

The concept of *sakdi na* has been the subject of much debate among scholars. Some have argued that it was similar to the feudal system that had existed in Europe in the Middle Ages, while others take the concept as reinforcing regal power rather than dividing ownership as with land granted in perpetuity. Given the divine concept of kingship, which the Ayutthaya kings adopted from the Khmer, and the fact that the monarchy held a monopoly on land ownership, a feudal ideology is unlikely. It is more probable that the *sakdi na* system worked whereby holders of land (and the associated manpower) owed the king a proportion of revenue from the land, as well as labour service, while the land, and the status it inferred, were temporary grants subject to the will of the king.

Trailok further greatly enhanced the effectiveness of government by separating administration into military and civilian divisions, each subdivided into numerous departments with specific responsibilities. The effectiveness of these administrative reforms, together with a strong economy founded on wet-rice cultivation, accounted to a large extent for Ayutthaya's ability to prevail in an era of unremitting and inconclusive warfare. The kingdom was recognized by China as Xian, a name the Portuguese would later interpret as Siam.

WAR WITH BURMA AND RELATIONS WITH THE WEST: 1488–1659

Ayutthaya reached the height of its power and glory in the 17th century, while the preceding century and the half century following were largely dominated by warfare with the Burmese, who eventually brought about the Thai kingdom's destruction. What most typifies Ayutthaya at its height, however, are its relations with the outside world, especially the European powers of the day, which added international trade to the control of manpower and wet-rice cultivation as the bases of unprecedented prosperity. This considerably strengthened royal power because the king held a monopoly on foreign trade, having first rights to purchase goods brought into the country at his own price, and similarly controlling the sale of outgoing commodities.

Commerce was already becoming a significant factor in the reign of King Trailok, when the port of Malacca on the Malay Peninsula, a vassal of Ayutthaya ruled by a Malay sultan, was an importer of rice from Ayutthaya and an exporter of Indian cloth and other goods. Trailok also took control of Tavoy and Tenasserim on the western coast of the Kra Peninsula, in a move, as David K.

Wyatt suggests, to gain access to the Bay of Bengal and the Indian Ocean. However, it was direct contact with Western traders in the 16th and 17th centuries that was to turn Ayutthaya into a major entrepot for East-West trade.

The reigns following Trailok, those of his son King Intharacha II (1488–1491, though he had previously reigned in Ayutthaya as Borommaracha III when his father ruled from Phitsanulok) and King Ramathibodi II (1491–1529),

saw the continued prosperity of Ayutthaya. In his short rule Intharacha II re-established Ayutthaya as the capital after Trailok's temporary relocation to Phitsanulok during his campaign against Lanna. On his death his 19-year-old younger brother contributed to Ayutthaya's greater glory with a building programme that included the construction of a number of Buddhist monuments. The most spectacular of these was a 16-metre (52-foot) high Buddha statue covered with more than 170 kilograms (375 pounds) of gold, the sight of which prompted the 17th-century French Jesuit Guy Tachard to remark: 'There is nothing to be seen but gold . . . It must needs touch one to the quick to see one single Idol richer than all the Tabernacles of the Churches of Europe.' The image was lost, however, in the 1767 Burmese destruction of Ayutthaya, when it was melted down for its precious metal.

The inland communications system was also enhanced by the digging of new canals and the improvement of existing ones, which were deepened to be able to take larger vessels. The major development in this respect was around present-day Bangkok, where a channel was cut between two canals to bypass the meandering course of the Chao Phraya, thereby shortening the river route between Ayutthaya and the sea.

Paralleling religious and civil advancements, the army was strengthened by Ramathibodi II, who remodelled the system of obligatory military service in 1518. The kingdom was divided into military divisions and subdivisions, and a conscription department was set up to administer the enrolment of all able-bodied men aged between 18 and 60, who were then liable for call-up. Two years' military training was required, after which all retainers (as they were known) effectively constituted reserve soldiers. Clearly, the majority would spend their lives in civil occupations without ever being called to arms, but the principle of universal service was recognized. Additionally, in a measure designed to create a better trained army, Ramathibodi II ordered a treatise on military strategy, tactics and martial arts to be compiled.

These were nonetheless relatively peaceful times, and while Lanna once again took the offensive by invading the area around Sukhothai in 1507, and Ayutthaya retaliated by taking Phrae the following year and, later, Lampang, Ramathibodi II was content with containment, appointing his eldest son as viceroy at Phitsanulok to secure the northern border. The son succeeded his father

as King Borommaracha IV (1529–1533) and continued the policy of appease-
ment, finally securing a peace treaty with Lanna shortly before his premature
death from smallpox.

The most significant event of the early 16th century, albeit low key to
begin with, was the arrival of the Portuguese, the first Europeans to establish
themselves at Ayutthaya. This was the great age of European voyages of discovery,
with Vasco da Gama having sailed around the Cape of Good Hope in 1498, and
across the Indian Ocean to engage in trade on the Malabar coast of India. Goa
was established as a Portuguese settlement, and in 1510 its viceroy, Alfonso
d'Albuquerque, sought to expand Portuguese influence eastwards and sent
a force of four ships to take Malacca, the rebellious vassal of Ayutthaya. The
Sultan of Malacca initially accepted the Portuguese but later tried to expel them,
prompting d'Albuquerque to attack with a fleet of 18 ships and capture the town
in 1511.

Aware of Ayutthaya's claims of suzerainty over Malacca, the Portuguese
quickly sent a mission to the Siamese capital, where it was well received and
a peace accord was concluded. The treaty was further extended by two later
missions, resulting in the Portuguese being granted right of residence in the kingdom, religious freedom and trade concessions, in return for which the Portuguese supplied firearms and mercenaries to use them. A visual record of this is
found in a few surviving Ayutthaya-period temple murals, which depict in the
traditional 'Victory over Mara' (forces of evil) scene somewhat comical-looking
Portuguese mercenaries armed with muskets.

On King Borommaracha IV's death his son, a child of five, was crowned
King Ratsada, but he reigned for just five months before a half-brother of his
father had him killed and himself crowned as King Chairacha (1534–1547). In
spite of the violence of the succession, the early years of the reign were peaceful
and Chairacha implemented further schemes to improve the navigation of the
lower reaches of the Chao Phraya River and open it to ocean-going traders. Also
at this time, the number of Portuguese residing in Ayutthaya was increasing and
Chairacha enrolled 120 of them to serve as a bodyguard, as well as to instruct the
army in musketry. It was a timely military build-up as war with both Burma and
Lanna was looming.

Burma had for some time been fragmented, divided principally into three main kingdoms: the largely Shan-controlled Ava in the north, the Mon state of Pegu in the south and, located roughly equidistant between them, the Burman kingdom Toungoo. Benefitting from the rivalries that beset Ava and Pegu, Toungoo remained quietly secure before exerting its authority during the reign of King Tabinshwehti (1531–1550) and crushing Pegu in the late 1530s.

This unification augmented Tabinshwehti's wealth and manpower, thus posing a direct threat to Ayutthaya, and Chairacha reacted quickly. During the war with Pegu, Tabinshwehti had occupied the town of Chiang Krai (or Chiang Kran), near Moulmien, which was at the time subject to Ayutthaya. In response Chairacha attacked with a strong army that included Portuguese mercenaries and utterly defeated the Burmese in 1538, expelling them from Thai territory. Chairacha may have thought his victory had quashed any Burmese designs on his kingdom, but it was to trigger a long and bitter enmity between the two countries, resulting in brutal wars and great suffering for both nations.

Wars were fought largely to take land and, most especially, manpower (a vital resource for both agricultural production and military might), but between the Thais and the Burmese there was also the vying for the title of *Cakkavatin*, meaning 'Universal Monarch', the ideal emperor, as described in Buddhist texts, who rules with justice over all people. Only one *Cakkavatin* was possible at any one time.

Before he went on the offensive against the Burmese, Chairacha was more concerned with Lanna. It was close to collapsing under the strain of bloody dynastic struggles and thus potentially falling prey to either the Shans of northern Burma or the Lao of Lan Sang. Between 1545 and 1547 Chairacha led two campaigns against Chiang Mai, but failed on both occasions to take the city; he died shortly after returning home from the second expedition.

Ayutthaya was now plagued by dynastic strife as violent as that of Lanna. Chairacha had reputedly been in ill health for some months before his death, but 16th-century Portuguese adventurer and writer Ferñao Mendes Pinto claimed that he was poisoned by his concubine, Princess Si Sudachan (there was apparently no wife who ranked as queen), which could well have been the case given the woman's subsequent murderous machinations.

The potential heirs to the throne of Ayutthaya were Chairacha's two sons, both born of Si Sudachan, and a younger half-brother, Prince Thianracha. The elder of the sons was made King Yot Fa (1547–1548) at 11 years old, with his mother acting as regent, while Thianracha, realizing that trouble was brewing, wisely retired into the Buddhist monkhood. Si Sudachan then took a minor court official, given the title Khun Worawong, as her lover (by whom she had a daughter), and became determined to make him king. Nobles who opposed her plan were eliminated – mostly stabbed in the back if Pinto is to be believed. Finally she had Yot Fa poisoned and raised Worawong to the throne (usurper June–July 1548). A group of outraged leading nobles formed a conspiracy and acted quickly, capturing Worawong, Si Sudachan and their infant daughter in an ambush and beheading them on the spot. The conspirators then approached Thianracha with an invitation to take the throne, which he accepted; he left the monkhood to be crowned King Chakkraphat (1548–1569).

Believing that Ayutthaya was weakened by the bloody dynastic upheaval, the Burmese decided to attack. Scarcely six months after Chakkraphat's coronation King Tabinshwehti went on the offensive, leading an army that according to some accounts numbered 300,000 men, 3,000 horses and 700 elephants. The Burmese entered Siam via the Three Pagodas Pass and pushed on through Kanchanaburi and Suphanburi, meeting little resistance on the way, and encamped close to Ayutthaya. The war was short-lived, though not without its epic moments.

89

QUEEN SURIYOTHAI IN THE BURMESE WAR

During one of the Thais' first forays in the war, intended as a test of the strength of the Burmese forces, King Chakkraphat, mounted on a battle elephant, led the army outside the besieged city. The story goes that Queen Suriyothai was fearful for her husband's safety; clad in men's armour and similarly mounted on elephant back, she accompanied the Thai troops. At one point Chakkraphat attempted to engage the Burmese commander in single-handed combat, but his elephant stumbled at a crucial moment, putting him at a severe disadvantage. Seeing the danger, Suriyothai forced her elephant between the two combatants, so saving the king but herself receiving a mortal wound. The event remains renowned in Thai history, and ever since Suriyothai has been held as one of the nation's greatest heroines. After the war Chakkraphat raised a *chedi* in her honour on her cremation site at Wat Suan Luang Sopsawan in Ayutthaya. Nothing remains of the temple although the *chedi* survives, albeit in restored form. Such is Suriyothai's lasting fame that in 2001 her story was brought to the big screen in epic style in the biggest budget film in Thai film-making history. The glorious tale is derived from various chronicles written long after the event and there are doubts as to its basis in fact. Nonetheless, Queen Suriyothai has in popular belief come to epitomize the qualities of bravery, love and wifely devotions.

LEFT
The Phra Chedi Sri Suriyothai was built in Ayutthaya by King Chakkraphat in honour of his valiant queen.

OPPOSITE
A memorial park outside Ayutthaya features a large statue of Queen Suriyothai wearing full battle dress and riding a war elephant.

91

Thai heroics aside, the Burmese were unable to breach Ayutthaya's defences, and with food supplies running short Tabinshwehti decided to withdraw. In the course of the retreat he managed to capture Chakkraphat's eldest son, Prince Ramesuan, and his son-in-law, Maha Thammaracha, viceroy of Phitsanulok, and negotiated their release on the condition that the Burmese army should be allowed to retire unmolested.

The Burmese withdrawal left Chakkraphat with no illusions that the threat had passed, and he wisely set about preparing for a second invasion. In 1550 work was begun on replacing Ayutthaya's old earthen ramparts with brick walls and digging an additional outer moat. Fortifications at Suphanburi, Lopburi and Nakhon Nayok were dismantled since these outlying towns were difficult to hold

and, if taken, could serve as enemy bases, although the defences at Phra Pradaeng, at the mouth of the Chao Phraya River, were strengthened as it guarded access from the sea. At the same time the navy's fleet of river warships was enlarged and improved, military conscription was reviewed, and the supply of arms and armaments, not least battle elephants, was boosted.

A second Burmese invasion was delayed, however, due to internal problems. Soon after his return home Tabinshwehti succumbed to excessive drinking and was assassinated when he became mentally unfit to govern. He was succeeded by his brother-in-law, Bayinnaung (1551–1581), who managed to quell what had become a chaotic situation, bringing rebellious vassal states into line and subsequently going on to conquer Upper Burma, followed by Lanna in 1558. With their power considerably increased by these conquests, the Burmese once again turned their attention to Ayutthaya.

In late 1563 Bayinnaung launched his invasion, electing to enter Siam from the north via Tak and not, as in 1549, through the Three Pagodas Pass. The northern towns fell quickly to the invaders. Maha Thammaracha, the viceroy of Phitsanulok and one of Ayutthaya's most high-born nobles, willingly or unwillingly submitted to the Burmese and accompanied their army south to Ayutthaya, which was besieged in early 1564 and pounded with cannon fire. Under such bombardment and facing superior forces, King Chakkraphat had no choice but to sue for peace and submit to Bayinnaung's terms, which included an oath of royal friendship and Chakkraphat's son, Ramesuan, given as a hostage.

This humiliating submission to the Burmese was not the end of Ayutthaya's woes. In an ironic turn of events the governor of the southern state of Pattani had raised an army to aid Chakkraphat, but finding that he had arrived too late sought to profit by turning traitor and plundering the king's palace. The rebellion was quickly put down, although it was yet another indication that the threat of instability remained ever present in the Thai world.

Chakkraphat had also lost the opportunity of forging an alliance with Lan Sang. The Lao King Setthathirat, who had recently moved his capital from Luang Prabang to Vientiane, requested one of Chakkraphat's daughters, Princess Thepkasatri, to be his bride. After initial reluctance Chakkraphat agreed, and sent the royal lady off to Vientiane in the company of a large retinue. Unfortunately, she never arrived because Maha Thammaracha, the renegade viceroy

OPPOSITE
Three Pagodas Pass, on the present-day border between Burma and Thailand and marked by its small eponymous monuments, was one of the classic invasion routes used by the Burmese in their wars against Ayutthaya..

A statue of Burmese King Bayinnaung, Ayutthaya's greatest adversary in the 16th century, stands in Thailand's modern northern border town of Mae Sai.

of Phitsanulok, had heard of the proposed marriage that would have linked the royal houses of Ayutthaya and Lan Sang and warned the Burmese. They duly ambushed Princess Thepkasatri's party near Phetchabun and carted her off to Pegu. Angered as well as humiliated, Setthathirat and Chakkraphat attempted retaliation but failed; Vientiane was even besieged for a while by the Burmese until they decided to withdraw in 1565.

For the second time in his life Chakkraphat retired to a monastery and appointed his son, Mahin, as regent. It was a disaster. Mahin was totally ineffectual, and in 1568 Chakkraphat again took command of the kingdom as a third Burmese invasion loomed. He made a final bid to regain control of his northern territories, managing to take Phitsanulok but failing at Kamphaeng Phet. He returned to Ayutthaya an old and sick man, and died there in early 1569, little more than a month after King Bayinnaung had launched a huge offensive – his army boosted by Maha Thammaracha's Thai troops from Phitsanulok – and once more laid siege to the Thai capital.

Chakkraphat was succeeded by Mahin (January–August 1569), who proved as ineffectual a king as he had been a regent. The Thais nonetheless stubbornly resisted the Burmese, largely due to the efforts of Mahin's younger brother, Prince Si Sawarat, and were finally defeated only by a trick. Phya Chakri, one of the Thai hostages taken in 1564, was sent into the city by Bayinnaung, appearing as if he had escaped from the Burmese. King Mahin not only unsuspectingly accepted him, but also placed him in a position of authority, from which Phya Chakri was able surreptitiously to weaken Ayutthaya's defences and expose it to an all-out attack. The Burmese struck hard and Ayutthaya fell in August 1569.

THE STRUGGLE FOR DOMINANCE: 1569–1605

Bayinnaung placed Maha Thammaracha on the throne as vassal king (1569–1590), while Mahin was led off as a captive and died of fever shortly afterwards. Thousands of Ayutthaya's citizens and a vast amount of loot were also taken to Pegu, and the city's fortifications were dismantled. Subsequently, Burmese laws and institutions were imposed, notably *Dhammasat*, a Brahmanical code of jurisprudence that was grafted on to Thai Buddhist laws, and the Burmese era calendar, both of which were maintained until the Bangkok period. Historically, however, the Thais have been distinguished by resilience. Now, as again they would in 1767, they succeeded in rallying from catastrophic defeat; in time, Ayutthaya was to achieve unprecedented power and prosperity.

For all his treachery or, in a more charitable view, his pragmatism, Maha Thammaracha was not content to be Bayinnaung's puppet, and although his kingdom was for the next 15 years virtually a Burmese province, he strove to restore the fortunes of Ayutthaya. Weakened in population, wealth and defences, the city was vulnerable to its old foes after the Burmese army withdrew. The Khmers in particular saw opportunities, which they exploited by repeatedly raiding Thai territory between 1570 and 1587. The losses incurred – mostly in war captives – were debilitating, but Maha Thammaracha used them as an excuse to strengthen Ayutthaya's defences without alarming the Burmese. In 1580 the city's walls were rebuilt and extended, defensive canals were dug and canon were purchased from the Portuguese.

Although the reign of King Maha Thammaracha was more positive for the Thais than might have been expected in the circumstances, this period and beyond is dominated by Prince Naresuan – later King Naresuan. The elder son of Maha Thammaracha, Naresuan was born in 1555 and became embroiled in politics and war at a tender age, having been taken as a hostage by the Burmese in 1564 as a guarantee of his father's fidelity. Ironically, the six years he spent in Burma, as Thai historian Rong Syamananda writes:

> proved to be a blessing in disguise. Not only did it afford him undreamt-of opportunities to examine quietly the strengths and weaknesses of the Burmese in general, but it also led to his study of their language, character and art of war amid sons of princes and nobles in particular. He had the fortune of being the first foreign educated Thai prince.

A born warrior and possessed of exceptional intelligence, resourcefulness and courage, Naresuan did not squander his hard-won knowledge and skills. After his return home he trained his own small band of troops in new methods of warfare, especially in guerrilla tactics. These highly trained, very mobile groups were given such names as 'Wild Tigers' and 'Peeping Cats'. They later had telling effect in battles against the Burmese, whose forces were otherwise superior in numbers and equipment, besides benefitting from the logistic support of supply lines via Lanna.

Popularly known as the Black Prince, Naresuan returned to Ayutthaya in 1571 after Maha Thammaracha had pleaded for his release in exchange for one of his daughters, who was given in marriage to King Bayinnaung. Now aged 16, Naresuan was appointed *uparat*, heir to the throne of Ayutthaya, and made governor of Phitsanulok. Over the next few years he was wisely given a largely free hand in the affairs of state by his ageing father. He more than proved his valour and military skills in a number of engagements against invading Khmer forces, as well as his regal standing when, in 1581, he represented his father in paying homage to King Nandabayin on his accession to the Burmese throne following the death of his father, Bayinnaung.

BELOW

King Naresuan the Great is honoured by an imposing modern memorial of marble and granite located a short distance north of Ayutthaya and featuring an equestrian statue of the monarch, along with engraved pictures illustrating episodes from his reign.

Soon, however, the Burmese came to view Naresuan as a potentially dangerous enemy. In 1584 Nandabayin requested Naresuan's help in suppressing a rebellion in Ava and secretly planned to have him ambushed on his way to join the campaign. The plot failed, reputedly because the two Mon chiefs, Kiet and Ram, who were sent to kill Naresuan, baulked at the idea and revealed the plot to the Thai prince. Naresuan then ritually renounced Ayutthaya's subjection to Burma. He levied troops among the Mon to reinforce his army, and marched back to Phitsanulok and on to Ayutthaya. Alarmed by this open act of defiance, Nandabayin made repeated attacks against Naresuan between 1585 and 1587, but all were to no avail. On the death of Maha Thammaracha in 1590, Naresuan was crowned king (1590–1605).

King Naresuan continued to face repeated Burmese invasions led by their crown prince, Mingyi Swa, and so readily repelled them all that Nandabayin became fearful for the security of his empire and decided on a final all-out push to subdue Ayutthaya, launching a major offensive in December 1592.

OPPOSITE
Elephants were the battle tanks of the Ayutthaya period, carrying kings, princes and generals into combat mounted on a howdah and armed with a variety of lances and other weapons.

BELOW
Statue of King Naresuan engaged in elephant-back combat. Typically, there was a soldier at the front to guide the elephant, leaving the king or general in the middle free to fight, protected by another soldier to the rear.

OPPOSITE

The Phra Chedi Chai Mongkhon ('Chedi of the Auspicious Victory') in Ayutthaya commemorates King Naresuan's victory over the Burmese in 1593.

Again under the command of Mingyi Swa, the Burmese crossed the Three Pagodas Pass. They reached Suphanburi without resistance, were joined there by a second army coming from the north and intended to march on Ayutthaya. Naresuan was more than prepared; he had been on the point of leading a campaign against the Khmer capital at Lovek, and on learning of the Burmese invasion led his already mustered troops out of Ayutthaya to meet the enemy in open country. Facing superior numbers, Naresuan decided against a direct attack and took up a strong defensive position at Nong Sarai, a few kilometres from the present-day city of Suphanburi, to await a Burmese assault.

Naresuan sent forward a small vanguard with orders to reconnoitre but not to attack. These orders were ignored and the Thais suffered heavy losses. Naresuan refused to send up reinforcements and instead held his main force steady while the Burmese, spurred on by their initial triumph over the Thai vanguard, rushed madly forwards. Having drawn the enemy into the position he wanted, Naresuan and his younger brother, Ekkathotsarot, both mounted on war elephants, charged into the midst of the Burmese. According to Thai chronicles, when Naresuan spotted Mingyi Swa he challenged him to one-on-one combat, saying, 'My brother, why do you hide yourself in the canopy of shadows? Let us fight the elephant battle for the honour of our kingdoms.'

In what has become a highly romanticized episode in popular Thai history, the fight was short and bloody. The two elephants were driven towards each other. Mingyi Swa slashed wildly at Naresuan with his war scythe and scored a glancing blow, but in doing so his body was laid open to a fatal sword thrust by the Thai king. Their crown prince slain, the Burmese fell into disarray and fled, suffering heavy casualties in their retreat.

VICTORY COMMEMORATED

At the conclusion of the war with the Burmese Naresuan had two *chedis* erected to commemorate his victory against the Burmese. The first was built at the site of his single-handed combat on 18 January 1593, but in subsequent centuries it was neglected and forgotten; it was not rediscovered until the early 1900s and was later restored. Today, an annual festival is held here on Royal Thai Armed Forces Day, which includes a re-enactment of Naresuan's triumph. A second, much larger *chedi*, named Phra Chedi Chai Mongkhon ('Chedi of the Auspicious Victory'), was built in Ayutthaya at what was then called Wat Chao Phaya Thai, but was later renamed Wat Yai Chai Mongkhon after the large (*yai*) Naresuan monument that still dominates the temple today.

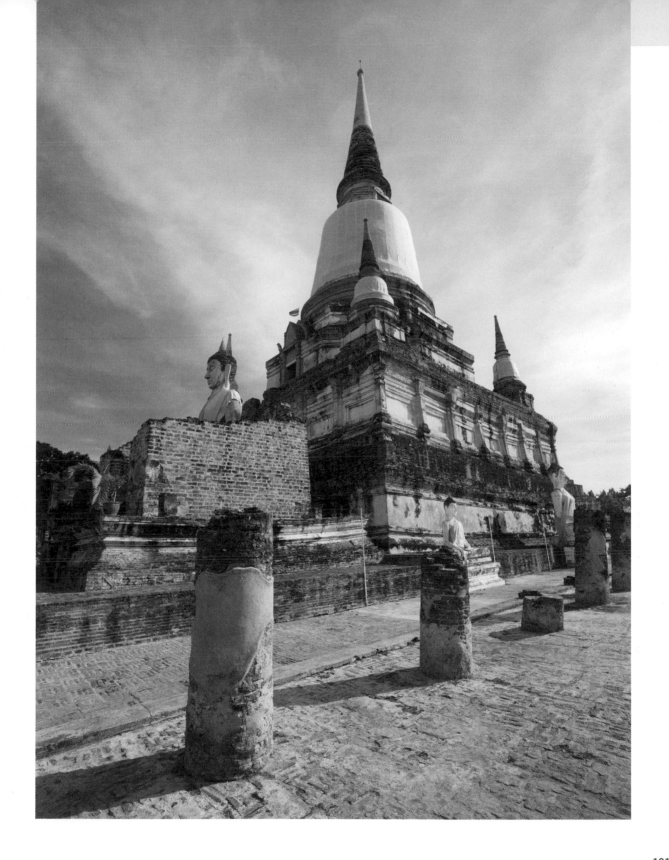

Naresuan's triumph ended the Burmese threat, making Ayutthaya the region's dominant force. Confidence had been restored and was underscored by largely successful military campaigns, naval as well as army, conducted during the remainder of the reign against both the Khmers and the Burmese, as well as by bringing Chiang Mai once more under Ayutthaya's dominance.

Internally, Ayutthaya was strengthened by administrative reforms. Perhaps mindful of his father's past treachery, Naresuan centralized control by ending the long-held practice of appointing royal princes as provincial governors and instead assigning court officials charged with carrying out the king's commands. Princes and other bluebloods were now retained at court, where a close eye could be kept on them. Additionally, a new decree gave the king at least a theoretical monopoly on manpower, whereby all male 'free' commoners, *phrai som*, became *phrai luang* who were required to undertake six months' corvee in either the army or the service of local officials.

Notwithstanding these changes, civil administration remained loose and Ayutthaya's direct control was never extensive beyond the capital. That said, while most of the major cities throughout the kingdom had their own ruling families, they were at the same time 'unquestionably emboxed within Ayutthaya's sphere of influence', in the words of historians Chris Baker and Pasuk Phongpaichit. The capital itself rose to unparalleled pre-eminence in the 17th century as the largest, grandest, richest and most cosmopolitan city in Southeast Asia, to some Western travellers' eyes outshining the European capitals of the day.

TRADE AND INTERNATIONAL RELATIONS: 1605–1656

Naresuan's renown as a warrior tends to overshadow his other accomplishment, specifically in fostering trade and international relations, most notably in maintaining diplomatic contacts with China and signing a treaty in 1598 with the Spanish, who had taken the Philippines. Moreover, in his conflict with the Burmese Naresuan did not seek a final knock-out blow once Ayutthaya itself was safe; rather his main aim was to secure the ports of Mergui, Tavoy and Tenasserim in southern Burma that gave access to the Indian Ocean and hence to international trade routes.

'With international trade,' writes David K. Wyatt, 'came diplomacy and the flow of political intelligence and new ideas. All these sources of strength, however, might have remained only potentialities without the wisdom and statecraft to maximize the advantages that might be gained from them. Naresuan and his successors made the most of them.'

The 17th century was to be Ayutthaya's century, arguably the most glorious period in Thai history, politically, culturally and most especially commercially. It

OPPOSITE

A row of Buddha images at Wat Yai Chai Mongkhon, one of Ayutthaya's oldest monasteries, which was restored by King Naresuan when he constructed his 'Auspicious Victory' chedi in the temple's compound.

was largely an era of peace and the nation, its finances depleted by decades of war, concentrated on reviving prosperity through trade.

King Naresuan died of a carbuncle at the comparatively early age of 50 (almost inevitably while conducting a military campaign, this time in the Shan States) and was succeeded by his brother, King Ekkathotsarot (1605–1610 or 1611). Having been a capable general to his brother, Ekkathotsarot now devoted his short reign to reorganizing finances, principally by levying new taxes on, it is believed, shops and markets, which were probably the first money taxes as opposed to payment by tribute. This, claims W. A. R. Wood, gave him the reputation of being a 'covetous man', although that seems scarcely justified when there was a legitimate need to replenish national coffers that had been greatly reduced by earlier warfare.

A more significant character trait was Ekkathotsarot's reputed favourable attitude towards foreigners, whether by inclination or merely the acceptance of fact, as Ayutthaya, now at peace, was looking increasingly attractive to other nations. The Dutch had established a 'factory', or trading station, in the southern port of Pattani, a Malay state under Thai rule, and in 1608 their first ships arrived at Ayutthaya. They were well received and in the same year Ekkathotsarot sent a diplomatic mission to the Netherlands, this being the first recorded visit of Thais to Europe. The Japanese were settling in Ayutthaya in significant numbers and were granted their own settlement by Ekkathotsarot, who maintained cordial relations with the Shogun of Japan through the exchange of letters and presents. Most of the Japanese engaged in trade, though some entered the king's service as royal guards.

In the following reign, that of King Song Tham (1610 or 1611–1628), a son of one of Ekkathotsarot's minor queens, came the first English traders, with the East India Company ship the *Globe* arriving at Ayutthaya in 1612 and bringing a letter of friendship from King James I of England and Scotland to the King of Siam. Like other foreigners, the English were favourably treated and permitted to establish a trading factory, although they encountered stiff competition from the Dutch and seem never to have fully capitalized on the opportunities. This was due partly to their ships not visiting Siam frequently enough, and particularly to the lamentable quality of the officers of the East India Company (in 1621, for example, the English agent at Ayutthaya was reported to be drunk every night).

The Church of San Petro in the Portuguese settlement at Ayutthaya is built over the excavated site of its 16th-century original. The Portuguese were the first Europeans to settle in Ayutthaya, where San Petro was one of three Catholic parishes.

By 1622 the English had decided to close their factories in both Ayutthaya and Pattani, and for the next 37 years they conducted no regular trade with the Ayutthayan kings. This situation considerably strengthened the position of the Dutch, who signed a treaty in 1617 with King Song Tham that gave them rights to the lucrative trade in hides.

The European presence was not limited to traders. Portuguese Catholic missionaries were settled in Ayutthaya, the first two Dominicans having arrived as early as 1555, with the first Jesuit, Balthazar de Sequeira, arriving in 1606. The Thais allowed freedom of religious practice, but although missionaries were active and built churches, converts were few.

As the 17th century progressed, Ayutthaya became more and more a truly cosmopolitan city, with the Chinese, and Persians and other foreign Muslims, who conducted most of the Asian trade, being joined by Europeans. As a contemporary French traveller remarked, 'It was a city of all the different peoples and the commercial centre of the universe where all the languages were spoken.'

W. A. R Wood suggests in his *A History of Siam* that Song Tham should be regarded as 'the first King of modern Siam, for it was under him that the habit of free intercourse with foreign Powers became well established'. This is partially justified, although as will be seen, events in the latter part of the 17th century reversed a trend that would not be fully revived until the mid-19th century.

What does beg the question is why there were no foreign designs to subjugate Ayutthaya. After all, the Portuguese had been aggressive in setting up their bases in Goa and Malacca. Thai historian Charnvit Kasetsiri believes Portugal saw Ayutthaya merely as a node in its spice network spanning the region. 'It wanted to set up shop here,' he says, 'rather than a colony ... And Ayutthaya was deep in the hinterlands, which made it difficult to access, unlike the port cities in other countries.'

Moreover, the Thais themselves lent no reason to any thoughts of colonization. They readily permitted foreigners the right to residence and to trade, and with control of the latter being a royal monopoly, they profited enormously. Additionally, while the royal court oversaw trade (administered by the specifically created post of *phrakhlang*, effectively a minister of finance and foreign affairs rolled into one), Thais were not entrepreneurs themselves and had no interest in becoming such. The society was divided broadly into royalty and nobility, and a

general population (apart from artists and artisans) engaged exclusively in agriculture. Where competition existed it was between different trading nations, not between foreigners and Thais.

While international trade was a dominant concern in 17th-century Ayutthaya, the role of foreigners was by no means limited to commerce. As Chris Baker and Pasuk Phongpaichit point out:

> The court made use of these peoples. It recruited Malays, Indians, Japanese, and Portuguese to serve as palace guards. It brought Chinese and Persians into the official ranks to administer trade. It hired Dutch master craftsmen to build ships, French and Italian engineers to design fortifications and waterworks, British and Indians to serve as provincial governors, and Chinese and Persians as doctors.

Such involvement of foreigners was a two-edged sword in that it both advanced Siam's profile on the international stage and complicated its internal politics.

There were ups and downs in foreign relations. Japanese palace guards had revolted on the accession of Song Tham, angered at the execution of a minister, their patron, for the role he had played in a court conspiracy, while neither the Dutch nor the English appeared willing to answer Song Tham's call for support in his campaign to regain control over Cambodia after it had declared its independence in 1618.

Song Tham was essentially a man of peace and appears to have accepted reversals, most notably the loss of control over Chiang Mai, which reverted to Burmese suzerainty in 1618. Before taking the throne he had been devoted to study and religious practice, and his reign is best remembered by Thais for the discovery of a huge Buddha footprint near Saraburi, which Song Tham had enshrined in a *mondop*. He inaugurated an annual pilgrimage to the site, a practice that continues today.

The death of Song Tham in 1628 triggered yet another bloody episode of succession. 'It is not a little remarkable,' notes David K. Wyatt, 'that virtually all successions to the throne of Ayutthaya in the 17th and 18th centuries were, at the least, irregular, and in many cases either disguised or real usurpations.' Part of the reasons why this was so, he suggests, was because 'Kings lacked the power to name their own successors, and blood was less effective a claim to the throne than strength.' Moreover, 'the crown was more worth fighting for than ever before', especially because its wealth and power were increased by expanded international trade.

The right of might certainly applies in the case of King Prasat Thong (1629–1656). Known originally as Phya Si Worawong, he was a cousin of Song Tham and an assertive man well versed in palace intrigues. On Song Tham's death he supported the succession of the eldest son, who became King Chettha (December 1628–August 1629). As Chettha was only 15 years old, Phya Si Worawong served as the power behind the throne. He had arrested and beheaded all those who opposed the new king, then set about manipulating the situation to his own advantage. Chettha became aware of the danger he faced, but any action he might have taken was pre-empted by Phya Si Worawong seizing the palace and arresting the king, who was subsequently executed.

Phya Si Worawong did not accept the throne at first and allowed Chettha's ten-year-old brother, Athittayawong, to be crowned king. He lasted barely a month before ministers saw him unfit to rule and appealed to Phya Si Worawong to assume the throne, which he did, taking the title Prasat Thong, 'Golden Palace'. (Athittayawong survived until 1637, when he was executed for involvement in an attempted rebellion.)

Prasat Thong was a usurper as he had no hereditary claim to the throne, although judgements differ as to the effectiveness of his long reign. Thai historian Rong Syamananda's opinion is that he was 'firm in dealing with foreigners and upheld national dignity and interests, despite the fact that he was beset with difficulties almost throughout his reign'. W. A. R. Wood, on the other hand, views him as 'one of those successful upstarts who succeeded, by sheer force of audacity, in impressing on others a false opinion of their merits'.

Contemporary opinions are equally conflicting. Successive Dutch agents in Ayutthaya during the 1630s had opposing views, one speaking highly of the king's reputation, the other being full of criticism. The discrepancy, however, may not be so much indicative of Prasat Thong per se as a reflection of the fluctuating nature of Dutch-Siamese relations. Indeed, the whole reign is marked by a rise in commercial activity combined with provincial and regional political problems – specifically troublesome neighbouring kingdoms and rebellious vassal states in the south – that impinged upon wider international relations.

In 1634, for instance, the Dutch sent ships to aid Ayutthaya troops in trying to put down a rebellion in Pattani; they arrived too late to prevent the defeat of Ayutthaya's forces, although the action was appreciated by Prasat Thong. A couple of years later, however, the king's ire was aroused when the Dutch opened a factory in what is today Cambodia. Nonetheless, in a reign full of revolts and murders, Prasat Thong tended to view Dutch support as a powerful tool that could be controlled by commercial rewards.

Broader, more balanced foreign relations were achieved by King Narai (1656–1688), another monarch whom Thai history honours with the title 'the Great', although before he took the throne there was a further period of disputed succession.

When Prasat Thong died in 1656 his eldest son, Chai, took the throne but was quickly done away with in a conspiracy led by his uncle, Prince Suthammaracha, and his younger brother, Prince Narai. Suthammaracha then seized the crown, but his reign lasted barely two months. In October 1656 he was attacked and killed by Narai after reputedly forcing his attention on his niece, although this could have been merely a pretext for Narai's ambitions.

THE REIGN OF KING NARAI: 1656–1688

The 32 years of King Narai's reign are dominated by Ayutthaya's relations with the West, which reached an unprecedented peak only to be suddenly and violently swept aside on the king's death. Thus, while the activities of the major European powers of the day colour the scene, they were ultimately played out against the backdrop of internal politics and court intrigue. Whatever Narai might have personally wished, the underlying instability of government and the nature of the Ayutthaya state itself were such as to inhibit any early and lasting flowering of international relations. It is important to note that international relations and the foreign policies pursued by Narai did have a profound impact on internal affairs and prompted various parties to pursue their own complex agendas. These eventually led to the so-called Revolution of 1688, which would alter the course of Thai history for the next 150 years.

With Narai taking the throne immediately following two royal executions in the space of three months, he may himself have felt somewhat insecure at first. However, his rule was consolidated in the time-honoured fashion of showing

A monument to King Narai the Great stands in the centre of Lopburi, the city that he chose as his second capital and where many of the important events of his reign took place.

military strength, and the early years of his reign were occupied by wars with Burma and Chiang Mai. Although Ayutthaya made no significant gains, the campaigns, at least one of which was led by Narai himself, were effective in reinforcing both Ayutthaya's status as a regional power and the king's personal authority.

With greater stability at court Narai was able to turn his attention to the Europeans, who were to overshadow all other events of the reign. International trade, controlled by royal monopoly, was obviously viewed as a lucrative means of restoring a treasury drained by wars, yet Narai showed a genuine interest in the West. He had an enquiring mind (astronomy, for example, was one of his interests) and a desire to learn from the Europeans. His political aims seem to have been little more than a desire to make his kingdom known abroad and for it to be recognized on the international stage. Referring to Narai in his *The Natural History and Political History of the Kingdom of Siam*, published in 1688, Frenchman Nicolas Gervaise remarked, 'Few sovereigns in the East had as many foreign friends as he did.'

While histories tend to focus on the Europeans at Ayutthaya, which is understandable given that the most eventful episodes of the period involved Westerners, the importance of Chinese traders should not be overlooked. They played a major role in commerce, but unlike the Europeans, were unobtrusive, took to local customs and very often married Thais. They were thus by and large absorbed into the population. This remained the case up to modern times, and with an agricultural society's natural aversion to commerce, the Chinese tended to comprise the majority of the merchant and (later) banking classes.

The spotlight during the Narai years is, however, focused on an unprecedented European presence. In 1661 the English East India Company returned to Ayutthaya after an absence of 37 years, and the French came in 1662. While the dominant foreign traders, the Dutch, had pulled out in 1663 in protest over changes in the terms of the royal monopoly, they were wooed back in the following year by Narai who, fearful that the kingdom would lose trade, offered a new treaty that included extra-territorial rights. Indeed, the freedom extended to Europeans was considerable and included more Christian missionaries being accepted, notably many of whom were French Jesuits.

The majority of the Europeans belonged to the East India trading companies of their respective nations, but there was also a growing number of private traders, particularly English ones, who were known scornfully as 'interlopers' and were in business for themselves. At the same time, Narai himself was something of a 'merchant king', strengthening the royal monopoly on trade and even fitting out his own ships, usually with foreign crews, to trade with India, Persia, China and Japan.

The growth of trade and a curiosity about the wider world provided the context for the most singular feature of the reign, Narai's appointment of a European as his chief minister and principal advisor. This was a man of Greek origin, born in 1647, with the name Constantine Gerakis, which means 'falcon' but is generally anglicized as 'Phaulkon'.

OPPOSITE

The ruins of Phaulkon's house in Lopburi show a substantial residence built of stone and brick and blending Thai and European architectural styles. This imposing residence was also used to host visiting foreign ambassadors.

THE INFLUENCE OF PHAULKON

As a young boy Phaulkon ran away to sea and worked as a sailor mostly on English merchant ships, living when ashore in London. He eventually arrived in the Orient on a vessel of the English East India Company, first going to the East Indies and later, in 1678, to Siam. Here he was aided by English friends Richard Burnaby, an agent of the English company, and the brothers George and Samuel White (the latter a colourful rogue who was soon to become a notorious privateer and ill-fated harbour master at the port of Mergui). Phaulkon set himself up as a trader at Ayutthaya.

An accomplished man who mastered the Thai language within a couple of years and was amazingly resourceful, Phaulkon was a complex and often contradictory character, possessed (for example) of both a captivating charm and an enormous arrogance. Above all he was driven by powerful ambition. Clearly a cut above the ordinary Western adventurer in Siam, Phaulkon soon attracted the attention of Narai. He entered government service in 1680, initially as an interpreter and accountant for the Phrakhlang. From 1683 until his death five years later he was the king's favourite, given the title Chao Phraya Wichayen, and would serve as the principal go-between during diplomatic exchanges between France and Ayutthaya. He became de facto the second most important man in the land – never before, or after, has a Westerner held such a position of authority in Thailand.

During the height of his career Phaulkon wielded incredible power, in the process amassing enormous wealth and living in great opulence. The ruins of his house can be seen at Lopburi, the city that Narai had made his second capital partly as a safe retreat from Ayutthaya and partly to satisfy his passion for elephant hunting in the surrounding countryside. These ruins illustrate Phaulkon's status, both in their size and in the fact that they were constructed in stone at a time when few buildings were, with the exception of temples and royal palaces.

The mainspring of events focusing on Phaulkon was Narai's fear of Dutch commercial and colonial intentions in the region and his desire to balance their power by courting another European faction. At one point Phaulkon, as the king's chief minister, turned to the English East India Company, but through a mixture of vacillation and the ineptitude of its agents it lost the initiative. Relations with the English were also soured by Phaulkon's arrogance in dealing with his former employers. This left France, which was at the time the all-powerful nation in Europe. Although lacking the commercial organization of the Dutch and the English, the French were building influence in Siam through the presence of Jesuit missionaries. These were befriended by Phaulkon, himself a Catholic convert after his marriage to a lady of Japanese and Portuguese extraction (he had originally belonged to the Greek Orthodox church and become a Protestant while serving with the English East India Company).

Here lies the nub of contention surrounding Phaulkon's intentions during the latter years of Narai's reign. Was his principle aim that of persuading Narai to convert to Catholicism, as many believe, or was he simply trying to walk an impossible diplomatic tightrope in order to win French support for Ayutthaya, and hence ensure a balance of power among the various European factions?

Narai's interest in the French predated Phaulkon's arrival on the scene, the king having looked favourably upon French Jesuits in Ayutthaya, who had provided technical assistance in royal construction projects. A reciprocation of the good will shown towards the Jesuits came in 1673, when ecclesiastical missions brought letters from Pope Clement IX and King Louis XIV of France, the latter of whom considered himself to be the Defender of the Catholic Faith. Subsequently, in 1680, Narai sent a mission to France. Although it never arrived and was presumably lost at sea, it did prompt the French to send a small commercial mission to Ayutthaya in 1682. Phaulkon, by now in Narai's trust, acted as interpreter for the mission and appeared keenly interested in pursuing the possibility of a Franco-Siamese alliance and the conversion of the king to Catholicism.

As the result of a second Thai mission to France in 1685, a high-level French mission, led by Chevalier de Chaumont, arrived at Ayutthaya in September 1685 with the main aim of securing the king's religious conversion. Narai received de Chaumont in October and a curious scene took place. The Frenchman had a letter for the Siamese monarch from Louis XIV, but he refused to present it in

OPPOSITE

A painting made much later from a contemporary engraving shows French ambassador Chevalier de Chaumont presenting a letter from King Louis XIV to King Narai. A prostrate Phaulkon, bottom left, is seen urging de Chaumont to raise the letter higher so that Narai should not have to lean down.

the customary style by kneeling. A compromise was reached; Narai appeared on a small balcony, while de Chaumont stood holding the letter on a plate, thus remaining below the head of the king, as strict custom demanded, while not having to kneel. However, he failed to hold the plate high enough for Narai to reach, despite promptings from the prostrate Phaulkon. To avoid an embarrassing confrontation with Gallic pride, the king reached down for the letter – at least this is how the scene was recorded in an engraving from which a much later painting was made, now on display at the Lopburi Museum.

Phaulkon was the organizer, translator and chief negotiator for the French mission, but there were to be few concrete gains as the Greek stalled and prevaricated out of, presumably, fear that the people of Ayutthaya would violently oppose their king's conversion, coupled with hope that a French commercial and defence alliance could nonetheless be somehow secured. With his experience of the Thai world it is hard to accept that Phaulkon could have genuinely believed a Catholic conversion was feasible. Instead he played a tricky and even devious diplomatic game, arguably with Ayutthaya's best interests in mind. For his part, Narai was pleased with the attention his kingdom was receiving from a major world power. He also showed himself receptive to learning about Catholicism, though more out of intellectual curiosity than any religious conviction. In the end a disgruntled de Chaumont returned to France in 1686, having gained only a draft commercial treaty with similar rights to those of other Europeans, and the right to station troops in the southern port city of Songkhla, a hotbed of rebellion against Ayutthaya that Narai wished to secure.

For the moment the aims of the French were in abeyance. While a second Thai embassy was sent to the court of King Louis XIV to pursue diplomatic relations, matters were temporarily overshadowed by two violent incidents at home, one threatening the stability of the reign and the other bringing Ayutthaya close to outright war with the English. In July 1686 Makassars, a small Muslim community originally from Sulawesi and not long settled in Ayutthaya, plotted to overthrow Narai and place one of his younger brothers on the throne on condition that he embraced Islam. Phaulkon learned of the plot, gathered a force of both Thai soldiers and European adventurers, and led a fierce pre-emptive strike that all but wiped out the Makassars, displaying in the process considerable personal courage. The incident further boosted Phaulkon's standing with Narai.

OPPOSITE
An inner gate of King Narai's palace in Lopburi. In the 19th century, King Mongkut restored parts of the palace. He added new buildings, one of which now houses the Phra Narai National Museum.

OVERLEAF
Ambassadors from Ayutthaya are pictured being received at Versailles by French King Louis XIV in a painting displayed in the Chakri Maha Prasat Throne Hall of the Grand Palace, Bangkok.

117

In the following year occurred what has become known as the Mergui Massacre, which was the culmination of increasingly deteriorating relations between the English East India Company and Ayutthaya. Located on the Andaman Sea coast, Mergui was a Thai port where, on Phaulkon's recommendation, Narai had appointed the Greek's old friends Richard Burnaby and Samuel White as, respectively, governor and harbour master. These two English rogues then proceeded to abuse their positions by carrying out virtual acts of piracy in the Bay of Bengal, in the process amassing considerable personal fortunes, largely at the expense of the English East India Company's trade with Golconda in southern India.

Frustrated and angered by Ayutthaya's apparent inability or unwillingness to rein in Phaulkon and the activities of his appointees, the English East India Company finally took action in April 1687 and claimed 65,000 pounds in damages from Narai, backing its demands two months later by sending two frigates to blockade Mergui. Burnaby and White attempted to appease the officers of the ships and temporarily calmed the situation. However, the population of Mergui, fearful of English intentions, took the offensive on 14 July and in the resulting affray some 60 Englishmen, including Burnaby, were killed. (White escaped by ship to England but did not live long to enjoy his ill-gotten gains.) Soon after the massacre Narai declared war on the English and appointed a French governor at Mergui.

Later in 1687 a second French embassy arrived at the court of Ayutthaya. It was an impressive affair headed by Claude Cébéret du Boullay, a director of the French East India Company, and Simon de la Loubère, who later wrote one of the most informed contemporary accounts of 17th-century Siam. It included six warships, about 500 troops, officials and Jesuit priests. Notwithstanding its magnificence, the embassy achieved little in spite of lengthy negotiations, conducted largely through Phaulkon, who this time made it clear that he did not support Narai's conversion to Catholicism and that any attempt to bring this about would be futile. A new treaty signed in December 1687 was no advance on that of 1685.

Matters came to a head shortly. Antagonisms at the court of Ayutthaya had been simmering for some time and there was a growing anti-foreign sentiment, directed especially at the French and their aim of converting Narai to Catholicism. Added to this were personal antagonisms against Phaulkon, who many envied for being Narai's favourite and despised for his arrogance. This gave rise to what may be described in today's terms as a 'nativist movement', though it was not as organized or as coherent as that might imply. The individual motives of its prime movers were mixed, personal ambition being among them. Heading this anti-foreign, anti-Phaulkon faction was Phra Phetracha, the influential Commander of the Royal Regiment of Elephants and childhood companion of Narai, along with his ruthless son Luang Sorasak. It all culminated in what has become known as the 'Revolution of 1688', a misleading title as it was not a revolution in that it did not change Ayutthaya's fundamental power structure.

Precipitating the action was the failing health of King Narai who, by March 1688, was terminally ill and lay dying at Lopburi. Courtiers had earlier persuaded him to appoint Phetracha as regent, while among obvious heirs to the throne were Narai's two brothers, Chao Fa Aphaithot and Chao Fa Noi, as well as an adopted son, Phra Piya. All three were suspect, having been variously implicated, rightly or wrongly, in the Makassar rebellion, and Phetracha's first move was to have Phra Piya killed. Later, shortly after the death of King Narai on 11 July 1688, Sorasak arranged the murders of Chao Fa Aphaithot and Chao Fa Noi. This left Phetracha little choice but to take the throne himself, whether he desired it or not.

Before that happened Phetracha settled Phaulkon's fate, having him arrested for treason, tortured to discover (unsuccessfully) the whereabouts of the fortune he was supposed to have amassed and finally beheaded in a squalid night-time execution. He met his end bravely, denying to his last breath that he had betrayed his king. A larger than life character, he remains a controversial figure; it can be argued that he was a traitor in supporting French designs on Ayutthaya and promoting Narai's conversion to Catholicism, but equally it can be said that he, unlike other foreigners in the service of Ayutthaya, genuinely dedicated his un-deniable talents to serving the interests of his adopted king and country, and only an overweening self-confidence led him to follow an impossible political path.

Lastly, Phetracha put paid to the French. Their garrison in Bangkok, under the command of General Desfarges, was besieged by Thai troops, and after some token resistance they agreed to leave the country. Jesuit missionaries were kept hostage to ensure the departure of the French troops, but were released shortly afterwards.

What persecution of foreigners there had been largely abated once the French had left, and although there was certainly a xenophobic element to the

LEFT

Taking 12 years to build and with French architects contributing to the design, King Narai's palace in Lopburi is today part ruins and part 19th-century restorations that are meticulously maintained and offer intriguing insights into 17th-century court life.

Revolution of 1688, it was motivated more by fear of the traditional power structure being undermined than fear of foreigners per se. Phaulkon was a foreigner, but it was his unprecedented rise to power that triggered alarm. Moreover, not all foreigners were expelled and – for example – Phetracha even signed a new treaty with the Dutch, who continued to trade more or less as before. There was no distinct policy of national exclusion and trade continued to have importance, particularly that with China. However, the dynastic change in 1688 did effectively close the kingdom to any significant relations with the West. The nation reverted to being introspective and preoccupied with internal conflicts.

As for King Narai himself, he is generally regarded as one of the greatest Thai monarchs. His long reign was in many ways an accomplished one, although he is most noted – and blamed by some – for an ambitious policy that ultimately failed. He was the first Thai king to recognize the value and need for development and progress through international relations. His rule coincided with the culmination of the first big wave of European interest in Southeast Asia. He was determined to reap benefits while attempting to safeguard his nation's sovereignty, doing so by skilfully playing off the Dutch against the English and the French against the Dutch in order to prevent any one power from gaining ascendancy. In this he was 200 years ahead of his time, and it was not until the mid-19th century that King Mongkut succeeded in establishing international trade along stable and mutually beneficial lines. It could be argued that Narai was ultimately defeated not by his own ambitions but by conservative elements at court, which illustrates the nation's as yet unpreparedness to deal with the wider world.

DECLINE AND FALL: 1688–1767

Once rid of foreign political influence, King Phetracha (1688–1703) showed no desire to pursue any hostilities against either the French or the English East India Company. The door had been shut and that was sufficient. Besides, he had to contend with the usual usurper's problems of securing his position and dealing with internal squabbles and intrigues. One of his first acts after taking the throne was to marry both Narai's sister, Princess Yotathip, and his daughter, Princess Yotathep, thereby bringing to the dynasty at least some legitimate royal blood.

Phetracha nonetheless had to deal with several challenges to the throne, mostly by imposters who claimed to be heirs of King Narai. In 1690 a rebellion broke out in Nakhon Nayok, to the east of Ayutthaya, led by Thammathian, who had once been an attendant of Chao Fa Aphaithot, one of Narai's murdered brothers, and now claimed to be the prince himself. He attracted a number of followers and advanced on the capital, but the rabble army was defeated and fled in disarray, while Thammathian was captured and beheaded.

Not long after Phetracha was faced with rebellious governors at Khorat, to the north-east, and Nakhon Si Thammarat in the south, who refused to acknowledge him as monarch. Both were finally defeated, but only after two years of putting up stiff resistance against several expeditions sent to take their cities. Peace did not last long, however, and Khorat again rose in revolt in 1698, this time led by Bun Khwang, a visionary fanatic claiming to be Narai's brother, as well as to possess supernatural powers. It was a bizarre affair and it was to be nearly two years before Bun Khwang and his original 28 followers were caught and executed.

Thus most of Phetracha's reign was occupied with putting down rebellions, thwarting plots and eliminating challenges to his legitimacy. He was described by F. H. Turpin in his 18th-century account, *A History of the Kingdom of Siam up to 1770*, thus: 'Phetracha, seated on a throne defiled with the blood of the royal family, combined in himself all the talents of great men with all the vices of the vilest scoundrels.' He was not, however, as bad as some have tried to make out. As a tough and rough old soldier he was simply dealing with circumstances, and as has been seen he was by no means Ayutthaya's first usurper. Moreover, many view him as a national hero who saved the nation from falling into the clutches of the French.

A much less positive picture can be painted of Phetracha's son and successor, Sorasak. As part of his attempt to establish the dynasty, Phetracha had elevated relatives to royal rank. Sorasak was made *uparat*, occupying the Palace of the Front, and was thus seen, certainly by himself, as heir apparent. However, Phetracha had two other, younger sons, Phra Khwan and Trat Noi, born respectively to Narai's mother and daughter and thus being of royal blood. The former was especially popular and seemed the likely successor to the throne. Fearful of this, Sorasak, already well practised in the art of eliminating potential rivals, enticed the 14-year-old Phra Khwan into a trap and had him clubbed to death. The plan almost backfired when Phetracha, on his deathbed in 1703, was so outraged at the murder of a beloved son that he proclaimed his nephew, Prince Phichaisurin, as his successor. But it was not to be. When Phetracha died, Phichaisurin, knowing only too well his fate if he took the throne, wisely handed over the reins of power to Sorasak. He was crowned King Suriyentharathibodi, although he is better and more appropriately known as King Suea, 'King Tiger' (1703–1709).

With all possible opposition already done away with, the six-year reign of King Suea was peaceful and uneventful save for – according to Turpin – a brief period of drought and famine. The monarch was thus able to spend his time indulging in his favourite pastimes of boxing (he is reputed to have travelled the country in disguise challenging all comers), hunting, fishing and pleasures of the

flesh, in so doing earning a reputation for cruelty, intemperance and depravity. One instance of mercy, however, has passed into Thai legend and has been portrayed in a modern play and film. The story is that of Norasingh, the coxswain of the royal barge who one day unavoidably allowed the boat to run aground, smashing its prow. The penalty at the time for such an offence was death, but in a rare moment of pity King Suea pardoned Norasingh, only to hear the latter insist on his punishment so that his honour and the law would be upheld; he was duly beheaded. A small shrine honouring the coxswain was later erected at the site of the incident on the banks of Mahachai canal.

His life shortened by his indulgent ways, King Suea died in 1709 at the age of 45 and was succeed by his eldest son, Prince Phet, who took the title King Phumintharacha, but was popularly known as King Thai Sa (1709–1733). The next 24 years were by and large peaceful, and the only major political event of the reign was in 1720, when Ayutthaya was drawn into involvement in the internal affairs of the Khmer kingdom. Some years before King Thommoreachea of Cambodia had been deposed by his uncle, Ang Em, who had secured the aid of the Vietnamese. In 1720, at the bequest of the exiled monarch, King Thai Sa sent both a land and a sea expedition to restore Thommoreachea to the throne. The naval force, under the command of the Phrakhlang, was defeated, but the body of Ayutthaya's forces led by Phraya Chakri was more successful and managed to advance to Udong, the then Khmer capital. There was, however, to be no victory for Thommoreachea as Ayutthaya accepted an annual tribute under vassalage and allowed Ang Em to remain king. What makes the event notable is that it marks the development of a pattern of Thai and Vietnamese wrangling over the Khmer lands of what is today Cambodia that would later become typical.

Otherwise, King Thai Sa spent most of his reign expanding commercial relations with China, which resulted in a significant growth in the export of Thai rice and the number of Chinese engaged by Ayutthaya to conduct the trade. He also embarked on the improvement of internal waterway communication with the construction of several new canals and the completion of Mahachai canal, where the luckless Norasingh had crashed King Suea's barge. Thai Sa is additionally known for building and restoring a number of Buddhist temples, as well as for constructing a *wihan* to enshrine the Buddha image at Wat Pa Mok. The image is one of the principal sights in Ang Thong province.

OPPOSITE

The 22-metre (72-foot) image of the Reclining Buddha at Wat Pa Mok in Ang Thong province is enshrined in a wihan constructed by King Thai Sa in the early 18th century.

127

Thai Sa's reign proved to be just an interval of calm in this otherwise stormy dynasty. His expected successor was his younger brother, Prince Phon, whom he had appointed as *uparat*, but he also had three sons, Naren, Aphai and Paramet. Before he died in 1733, he oddly expressed the wish for Aphai to succeed him. A fierce struggle for the throne then broke out between all parties except Naren, who at the time was serving in the monkhood, and for a while Ayutthaya was turned into a battleground. Aphai, Paramet and their supporters occupied the royal palace, while Prince Phon made the Front Palace his power base. In the ensuing battle Prince Phon managed to defeated Aphai and Paramet in spite of his forces being outnumbered by roughly five to one, and so succeeded as King Borommakot (1733–1758). According to some accounts, Aphai and Paramet escaped by boat under the cover of darkness and went into hiding, only to be captured a week later and executed. (In Turpin's admittedly highly coloured account, more died in the civil war 'by the sword of the executioner than on the battlefield'.)

Most historians view the reign of King Borommakot as Ayutthaya's late golden age, a final flowering before the fall. It was a time of peace during which the arts, especially poetry, flourished (one of the king's sons and two of his daughters ranked among the period's most distinguished poets). Buddhism also enjoyed strong royal support, and Borommakot built or repaired 'so many temples that the skyline of Ayutthaya was totally remodelled', in the words of historians Chris Baker and Pasuk Phongpaichit. Such was the king's reputation as an upholder of the faith that in 1751 an embassy from Sri Lanka requested his help in purifying Theravada Buddhism in that country. Accordingly, a mission of Siamese monks was sent and succeeded in founding a new Ayutthaya-ordained sect of the Lankan monkhood. This was reinforced by a second Siamese mission in 1755 – given that Sri Lanka had long been considered the preserver of Theravada Buddhism, this highlights the Lankan's respect for the purity of the faith that Ayutthaya had kept.

Under Borommakot Ayutthaya's regional power was further underscored by its successful intervention in deposing and replacing the Khmer monarch on two occasions, in 1738 and 1749, the latter in an ongoing pattern of opposition to Vietnamese intentions in what is now Cambodia. With the Burmese, too, Ayutthaya played a diplomatic role, though one of neutrality, when the Mons

OPPOSITE
Ayutthaya's Wat Mahathat was restored by King Borommakot, who added four porticos to the main prang only a few years before the city was sacked by the Burmese. In spite of its ruined state the prang remains an impressive structure.

rebelled against Ava, the Burmese capital, and established an independent kingdom at Pegu in 1740. Burmese refugees from the conflict were given asylum at Ayutthaya, for which the king of Ava expressed his gratitude to Borommakot. Diplomatic missions were exchanged, but Ayutthaya had no wish to become embroiled in the Ava-Pegu conflict and maintained its neutrality while keeping a close watch on the turn of events.

An admirable personality in many respects, balanced and wishing to avoid conflict, Borommakot could nonetheless be severe when the occasion demanded. In 1755 he discovered that his eldest son and *uparat*, Prince Senaphitak, was carrying on an affair with one of his queens; such was his fury that he had both offending parties flogged to death.

With Prince Senaphitak having predeceased him, Borommakot was left with a choice between two younger sons as his successor. He thought the elder, Prince Ekkathat, did not possess the qualities of a ruler, so passed him over in favour of the younger, Prince Uthumphon, who duly became king on Borommakot's death in 1758. The succession was opposed by Uthumphon's three half-brothers, but their planned armed uprising was quickly thwarted and the three conspirators were arrested and executed. Even then, Uthumphon reigned for only a short time in April–May 1758, before ceding the crown to his ambitious elder brother, who took the title King Borommaracha but is more commonly known as King Suriyamarin (1758–1767).

Borommakot was to be proved correct in his estimation of his sons, and Suriyamarin turned out to be as ineffectual as feared, his reign ending in disaster. Yet again, internal conflict followed the succession and Borommaracha had first to contend with a plot to return Uthumphon to the throne. The plan failed, with Uthumphon retiring into the monkhood, but it showed a dangerous lack of support for the king among princes and officials, which weakened Ayutthaya just when it was about to face its greatest external challenge.

As noted, Ayutthaya remained a neutral bystander when the Burmese kingdom underwent political upheaval in the 1740s, but in the early 1750s the Mons were defeated by the Burmans under King Alaunghpaya, who reunited the country and restored Ava as the capital. Burmese attention now became focused on Ayutthaya, for various reasons. It had received a number of Mon refugees who, with the backing of Ayutthaya, could possibly attempt to retake Pegu for their capital, and also King Alaunghpaya most probably wished to assert his author-ity and the power of Ava, there being no better way to do so than to successfully take on a neighbouring state. Moreover, there was the example of conquests by earlier Burmese kings who Alaunghpaya, a dyed-in-the-wool warrior, would have doubtlessly liked to emulate.

In 1760 Alaunghpaya led an army south, taking Tavoy, Mergui and Tenasserim before heading up the peninsula to capture Phetburi, Ratburi and Suphanburi. Meeting scant resistance, and after receiving reinforcements, he marched on Ayutthaya and laid siege to the city. The relative ease with which this

Bang Rachan Memorial Park, opened in Singburi province in 1976, commemorates the Thai heroes who put up valiant residence against the Burmese, delaying their advance by some months before their final defeat of Ayutthaya in 1767.

invasion was carried out was due largely to the incompetence of the Thai leadership, coupled with the fact that the Thais had not been engaged in serious warfare for several decades and were thus ill-prepared to mount any effective defence.

The siege lasted one month and may have succeeded had not Alaunghpaya been seriously wounded when one of the Burmese cannon burst accidentally. With their commander unable to direct the offensive the Burmese were prompted to withdraw, and Alaunghpaya died during the retreat.

In spite of the alarm triggered by the 1760 siege, Ayutthaya failed to learn any lesson and seemingly relaxed after the immediate danger had passed. Ayutthaya's fortifications were repaired and strengthened, and weapons were stockpiled, but no effort was made to establish a more effective leadership, which remained weakened by officials split between those who supported Suriyamarin and those who would have Uthumphon returned to the throne.

Meanwhile Alaunghpaya's successors, King Naungdawgyi (1760–1763) and King Hsinbyushin (1763–1776), continued aggressive policies; by 1765 both Chiang Mai and Luang Prabang had been captured. The stage was now set for a final Burmese assault on Ayutthaya. It was to be a two-pronged advance, beginning in July 1765 with one Burmese force, its ranks swelled by troops from conquered Chiang Mai and Luang Prabang, moving south from Lampang and through all major towns down to Ang Thong, a short distance north of Ayutthaya. In September a second army marched from Tavoy, and after crossing the peninsula pushed north through Chumphon and on up to Phetburi. Joined by a third Burmese force that had crossed via the Three Pagodas Pass, it proceeded to take Ratburi and Suphanburi.

Both these Burmese marches were conducted with a ruthless single-mindedness, all opposition being viciously swept aside, either killed or taken as slaves, and most of the Thai population in the line of the Burmese advance fled into the jungle. Only at the village of Bang Rachan, in what is today Singburi province, was there any effective Thai resistance, with guerrilla groups managing to stall the northern Burmese advance for five months before being crushed by superior numbers.

By February 1766 a combined Burmese force of around 40,000 troops had laid siege to Ayutthaya. The Thais had hoped that the coming rainy season, which annually flooded the plain around Ayutthaya (traditionally an effective part of

the city's defences), would force the Burmese to withdraw, but they concentrated their forces on the higher ground and remained in place, on some occasions using boats to sustain military action. At one point King Suriyamarin offered to submit and become a vassal of Burma, but that was not the aim of the Burmese; their intention was the complete destruction of a rival capital.

As the siege continued conditions inside Ayutthaya deteriorated drastically, with the people suffering increasingly from famine and disease. Finally, at sunset on 7 April 1767, the Burmese launched an all-out onslaught, breached the walls of Ayutthaya and swarmed into the city. During the night and the days that followed Ayutthaya was torched, sacked and razed with a ferocity and thoroughness that had been spawned by the frustrations of a 14-month siege. The havoc wreaked was final and complete, and the magnificence of what had been the focus of the Thai world for more than 400 years was lost forever, its art treasures, literature and historical records looted or destroyed.

According to some accounts, King Suriyamarin managed to escape but died of starvation ten days later, while others hold that he was caught outside the city walls and killed by Burmese soldiers. Prince Uthumphon, other members of royalty and the nobility, together with thousands of ordinary Thais, were led away into captivity. Those who escaped the massacre struggled to survive as best they could. 'Afflicted with a thousand ills, some died and some lived on', as one witness later remarked.

6

BANGKOK
The Making of the Modern State
1767 to the Present

Resilience is a pronounced characteristic of the Thais, and never was it more apparent than in the aftermath of the fall of Ayutthaya. The Thai capital lay in ruins, but the physical destruction failed to undermine a sense of nationhood and the traditions – administrative, commercial and cultural – on which it had been built. Within just a few years of defeat by the Burmese the Thais had not only rallied and driven the enemy from the land, but had also rebuilt a kingdom and, after a brief interim, established a new capital and ruling dynasty, both of which exist today.

More surprising than the rapid recovery was the renewed strength the Thais found. This resulted from what began as a response to disaster but soon developed into expansionism, initially though military action and later by a revitalized sense of identity and purpose. Centralized Thai influence came to extend further into the north, south and east than previously. Although at first projected as a revival of Ayutthaya, with a physical recreation of Ayutthaya being the original intention in the building of a new capital, the Thai kingdom gradually evolved as something different, though without losing its defining 'Thainess'. The nation was not only larger, but also more stable and more assured, something that would become particularly apparent in the mid-19th century, when relations with the West gained fresh importance in the age of imperialism.

THONBURI INTERLUDE: 1767–1782

Emerging, as it were, from the ashes of Ayutthaya was General Phraya Taksin. A charismatic figure of half-Thai and half-Chinese descent, he had been governor of the important garrison town of Tak but was recalled with his troops back to Ayutthaya when the Burmese invaded. Here he fought in the city's defence until it became obvious that further resistance was useless, and he managed to break

OPPOSITE
An equestrian statue honouring King Taksin appears appropriately defiant amid the modern building and traffic congestion of today's Thonburi, now part of Greater Bangkok.

free and escape with a band of followers. He moved south-east, first to Chonburi then to Rayong, on the eastern seaboard, where he gathered more supporters and raised a small army that he successfully led against the governor of Chanthaburi, who had rebuffed his offer of friendship.

At this time, having systematically sacked and looted Ayutthaya, the Burmese withdrew their main force, leaving behind a garrison of only some 3,000 troops, and focused their attention on the north where a Chinese invasion threatened. With the kingdom in chaos, the country was subject to raids by bandit groups, although five different power centres were established and a degree of order began to emerge in separate regions. Of these power centres only one, at Phimai in the north-east, had any claim to royal legitimacy, being governed by a son of King Borommakot, but it was Taksin's base on the east coast, an area that remained relatively well populated and untouched by the Burmese, which emerged as the strongest.

In October 1767 Taksin led a force of 5,000 men up the Chao Phraya River and took Thonburi, on the west bank of the river opposite present-day

Bangkok, executing the port's Burmese-installed governor. He quickly moved on from this success to defeat the main Burmese garrison near Ayutthaya, thus taking back the city just seven months after its fall. However, Taksin made no attempt to revive the capital, partly due to its state of destruction, but also because he did not have sufficient forces to defend the city. Instead, he returned to Thonburi which, because it was a small town, could more easily be protected and also had the advantage of controlling seaborne trade up the Chao Phraya River.

Here, in late 1767, prominent officials who had rallied around him offered him the crown and he duly proclaimed himself monarch of the entire nation, as King Taksin (1767–1782). Without any royal legitimacy he had risen to

ABOVE
The Chao Phraya River, photographed here at the end of the 19th century, was Bangkok's focal point until development started to spread eastwards during the mid-20th century.

RIGHT
Wat Phra Kaeo, the main chapel of which was completed in 1784, stands within the walled complex of the Grand Palace established by King Rama I.

power not only through his military prowess and a charismatic leader's ability to win people over to his side, but also because, with his Chinese connections, he succeeded in gaining the support of Chinese traders who supplied desperately needed rice and other goods. He was thus able to restore some measure of prosperity, along with the safety of persons and property, prompting the contemporary observer F. H. Turpin to remark that: 'The Usurper justified his claims by his benevolence.'

While trade and changes in the economy were to be of increasing importance, Taksin was primarily a warrior king and his reign was focused on military campaigns against a motley collection of self-appointed provincial rulers – who included cadet members of the royal family, generals and even renegade monks – and on reconstituting the territories of the kingdom. After an initial failure to take Phitsanulok in 1768, over the next two years he succeeded in subduing Phimai, Nakhon Si Thammarat, Fang and, finally, Phitsanulok in 1770, as well as annexing western parts of what is now Cambodia. His biggest territorial success, however, came in the mid-1770s when, in alliance with Chao Kavila, he conquered Chiang Mai. Vientiane, in present-day Laos, also fell to the Thais in 1778, an event best remembered for the acquisition of the Emerald Buddha image which had been taken from Chiang Mai in the 16th century and would now be instated as the palladium of the Thai nation, shortly to be enshrined in Bangkok's Wat Phra Kaeo.

THE EMERALD BUDDHA

Not made of emerald but carved from a single piece of green jasper, the 66-centimetre (26-inch) tall statue of the Emerald Buddha (see page 140), dressed in one of three costumes changed according to the three seasons in a solemn royal ceremony, is the nation's most sacred image. Believed to be of great antiquity although its origin is unknown, the statue was discovered, according to a reliable chronicle, in 1434 in the northern city of Chiang Rai when lightning split open an ancient *chedi* and revealed an image covered with stucco which later flaked, exposing the true material beneath. Upon learning of this mysterious discovery, the King of Lanna ordered the statue to be brought to Chiang Mai, but the journey was unexpectedly protracted as the elephant bearing the image refused to travel the route. This was seen as an omen and instead the Emerald Buddha was taken to Lampang, where it resided for 32 years before finally being enshrined at Wat Chedi Luang in Chiang Mai. Later, in 1552, a prince of Chiang Mai removed the statue and took it to the *mueang* of Wiangchan (Vientiane), and it was not until 1778 that General Chakri (later King Rama I) defeated the Lao and brought the Emerald Buddha to the Chao Phraya delta, where it was later enshrined in the newly built Wat Phra Kaeo in Bangkok.

Phra Phutthayotfa, King Rama I, founder of the reigning Chakri dynasty and of Bangkok as the kingdom's capital.

OPPOSITE
Enshrined in Wat Phra Kaeo, the Emerald Buddha is the nation's most sacred Buddha image. It is clothed in three bejewelled costumes that are changed in a royal ceremony in accordance with the three seasons.

The early campaigns were led personally by Taksin, a skilled military tactician and a man of considerable courage, but in the latter years of his reign his leading generals played a greater role in the field. Prominent among them were two brothers, Thong Duang and Bunma, holding the titles of Chao Phraya Chakri and Chao Phraya Surasi. Aged respectively 30 and 24 at the time of the fall of Ayutthaya, the two were descendants of an established and well-connected noble family. Both had joined Taksin's forces early on, distinguishing themselves in various military campaigns, including the defeat of a Burmese counter-attack. By 1775 the elder, Chao Phraya Chakri, was given commanded of the Thai forces.

Taksin was less successful at holding court in Thonburi than he had been in leading his troops on the battlefield. He showed increasing signs of insanity, manifest most noticeably in a kind of religious mania, believing himself to be a reincarnation of the Buddha and meting out harsh treatment to monks who refused to recognize him as such. Matters came to a head in 1781, when rebellion broke out in Saraburi and Ayutthaya provinces. The attack was initially aimed at Ayutthaya's tax-farmer, a royal appointee, but it soon developed into a call for the overthrow of Taksin. The rebels advanced on Thonburi virtually unopposed, took the king prisoner and called on Chao Phraya Chakri, at the time leading a military campaign in Cambodia, to take the throne.

On learning of the events Chao Phraya Chakri called off the Cambodian expedition and quickly returned to Thonburi, accepting the crown on 6 April 1782, as King Ramathibodi (1782–1809). He was posthumously known as Phra Phutthayotfa, Rama I (Rama is the title by which the kings of the Bangkok period are most readily designated), with the name Chakri adopted for the dynasty. A council of leading officials unanimously condemned Taksin to death and he was executed, either beheaded like a commoner or, as popularly believed, in regal fashion by being tied in a velvet sack and beaten with a sandalwood club (this method ensured that neither was the royal personage directly touched, nor royal blood spilt). Taksin's end tends to overshadow his accomplishments, certainly in the eyes of his contemporaries, but his was an extraordinary reign in which, under his brilliant leadership, a defeated nation was restored to more or less its former boundaries within the space of just 15 years. He had little time to build any lasting monuments in Thonburi, although he is honoured there today in a rather dashing equestrian statue (see page 134).

THE FIRST THREE REIGNS: 1782–1851

King Rama I's major decision at the beginning of his reign was to create a new capital at Bangkok. This was a strategic move as Thonburi, being on the west bank of the Chao Phraya River, was exposed to possible attack from the old enemy to the west, Burma, while Bangkok, on the eastern side, could be more easily defended. Moreover, Bangkok's network of canals (there were no roads as such) replicated the island city that Ayutthaya had been.

The site chosen by King Rama I for his palace (the Grand Palace) was at the time occupied by Chinese traders who, with compensation, were requested to move a short distance downriver to Sampaeng, which is still today Bangkok's Chinatown. The building of the new capital began in earnest. Not only did the lost glory of Ayutthaya inspire the planning, but there was also a physical

ABOVE

Bangkok canal scene in the early 1900s. Known to foreigners as the 'Venice of the East', Bangkok was largely an aquatic city until well into the 20th century, and only gradually did paved roads come to replace canals as the main transportation links.

143

reconstruction in that bricks from the ruins of Ayutthaya were ferried down the Chao Phraya and used in the building of the city. However, although Ayutthaya did in many ways provide a model for Rama I's capital, a different and stronger Thai world was to emerge during the reign.

Rama I inherited problems created by Taksin's idiosyncratic later years, which had to be addressed, although he did maintain one important element established by Taksin and that was a strong link with the Chinese merchant elite. Like his predecessor, Rama I had blood connections with the Chinese, in his case on the distaff side of the family, and he used them to help develop Bangkok into a new commercial hub for Chinese merchants, so boosting rice exports.

LEFT
*Originally occupying the
site of what is now the Grand
Palace, Bangkok's Chinatown
was moved during the First
Reign a short distance
downstream, where it
remains today.*

OPPOSITE
*Although now congested
with traffic, Chinatown
has nonetheless managed
to retain its quintessential
identity for more than
200 years.*

In terms of problems inherited from Taksin's reign, the most urgent was religious reform. Taksin in his excesses had antagonized the monkhood, while at the same time Buddhism was seen to be in decay, a factor thought by some to have brought about the fall of Ayutthaya. Rama I thus initiated a number of laws designed to restore religious discipline, as well convening a council to overhaul the *Tripitaka*, the Buddhist 'bible', in 1788–1789. Most visibly, with much pomp and ceremony he enshrined the Emerald Buddha in the royal chapel of Wat Phra Kaeo, the main *bot* of which was completed in 1784.

Religious reforms were matched by a cultural revival which, with libraries lost in the destruction of Ayutthaya, is most emphatically exemplified in a new version of the *Ramakien* composed by Rama I in 1798. This was no mere translation of the Indian *Ramayana*, but rather an essentially Thai rendering of the epic tale that incorporated Thai and Buddhist ceremonial elements in order to preserve knowledge of Ayutthaya traditions.

The social structure, too, was consolidated under Rama I, and the noble families that had survived the fall of Ayutthaya, along with those elevated in reward for their support in the reconstruction of the nation, became established and played major roles in the administration. This marked the emergence of a new pattern in which the nobility was increasingly influential and the king, though still an absolute monarch, could in certain respects be seen as 'first among equals'.

TERRITORIAL EXPANSION UNDER KING RAMA I

Paralleling the re-establishment of religious and cultural patterns that underpinned Thai identity was a territorial and administrative consolidation of the nation. Rama I continued the military expansion initiated by Taksin and was extraordinarily successful in pushing the boundaries of the kingdom. In this he was ironically aided by the Burmese who, in 1785, launched a huge, five-pronged attack involving some 100,000 troops and targeting the south and north as well as Bangkok. The enormous danger to which the Thais were exposed was dealt with decisively by Rama I in a series of military actions that succeeded in repulsing the enemy. Hostilities were to continue sporadically for several more years, but the events of 1785 effectively signalled the end of the long-standing threat posed by the Burmese.

The result was not simply the successful defence of the kingdom: in repelling the Burmese on all fronts, Rama I had the opportunity and the incentive to exert greater control over the more distant provinces. Chiang Mai and the north were brought under Bangkok's control, albeit given a degree of administrative autonomy, while in the far south the Muslim Malay states of Pattani, Kedah, Kelantan and Trengganu had shown less resistance to the Burmese and were firmly brought under Thai suzerainty. Moreover, strengthened by his triumph over the Burmese, Rama I was free to turn his attention to the east, where he extended Thai dominance over much of present-day Laos and Cambodia, so making Bangkok the major regional player with the capability, via tributes, to draw on considerable manpower.

OPPOSITE

A city landmark, Bangkok's Wat Arun was initially developed by King Rama II and completed in the following reign, when its main tower was raised to its present height (variously measured as between 66.8 and 86 metres/219 and 282 feet) and the structure's surface was decorated with pieces of coloured Chinese porcelain.

Substantial commercial, cultural, religious and territorial developments distinguish Rama I's reign, although it is also important to appreciate two new aspects seen in the character of the Thai monarch, as David K. Wyatt has noted. First, Rama I saw a necessity to explain himself when making new laws and decrees, saying why as well as what; second, he was willing to share power with those closest to him. 'Together, he and they,' Wyatt writes, 'constructed a new empire that was significantly more powerful, more flexible, and more complex than Ayutthaya had previously been.'

Rama I died in 1809 at the age of 72 and was succeeded by his eldest son, Prince Itsarasunthon, who took the title King Phutthaloetla, Rama II (1809–1824). Although he was experienced in military and government affairs, it was almost inevitable that he would be overshadowed by the accomplishments of his father, and his reign tends to be viewed as a passive period. In one respect, however, his succession was historic in that it was a smooth and peaceful transition in marked contrast to the succession squabbles and often usurpation that were more the norm than the exception during the Ayutthaya period. Moreover this was the beginning of a dynasty that was to endure; it signalled a shift in emphasis from the reign of an individual to that of a continuing royal line, something that would add to the growing strength of the nation.

ARTISTIC ACHIEVEMENTS UNDER KING RAMA II

King Rama II is best remembered as a man of the arts. Several Bangkok temples were restored and embellished under him. Most famously, he initiated the construction of the iconic Wat Arun on the west bank of the Chao Phraya River; the temple was completed in the following reign. He did not, however, just initiate architectural works. He would also at times take an active role in their construction and, for example, a finely carved wooden door panel at Bangkok's Wat Suthat has been accredited to his workmanship.

A gifted all-round artist, Rama II's greatest love was literature and dance drama, and he excelled as a poet. He is recognized today as one of Thailand's greatest poets, having composed seven epic-verse dramas, the best known and still much admired being the *Inao*. This long tale, comprising 45 volumes in its original manuscript form, was a typically intricate story originating in Java, although Rama II's version is notable for its humour, its fine descriptive passages and, most interestingly, its portrayal of contemporary Thai manners and customs.

While the arts flourished, Rama II's reign was not without incident – there was war with Burma in 1810, antagonism with Laos and the long-standing vying with the Vietnamese for control over Cambodia. However, these were low-key affairs and the single most important event of the period was renewed relations with the West, the first significant contact since the Revolution of 1688.

In the late 18th and early 19th centuries, the British were again showing interest in Southeast Asia. In 1785 they had taken the island of Penang, off the coast of the Sultanate of Kedah, which was under Thai suzerainty; later, in 1819, they founded Singapore as a maritime trading hub. The impetus for opening Anglo-Thai relations came in 1821, when the Thais invaded Kedah having received reports that the sultan was plotting a rebellion. The British were drawn into the conflict when the sultan fled to Penang to seek their assistance, but they decided that the best solution to the chaos was to push for a commercial treaty with the Thais.

Accordingly, in 1821 John Crawfurd, formerly British resident at the Court of the Sultan of Jogjakarta, was appointed to head a mission to Bangkok. The Thais, however, were in no mood to negotiate and all that Crawfurd achieved was an official Thai recognition, nearly 40 years late, of Penang as a British possession. If not immediately fruitful, the mission did at least open a way for future bilateral negotiations. Crawfurd's *Journal of an Embassy to the Courts of Siam and Cochin China*, published in 1828, gave a detailed account of the Thais and their kingdom that greatly increased British awareness and understanding, and would be instrumental in facilitating future Anglo-Thai relations.

Of Rama II, Crawfurd wrote with not a little condescension that: 'the country prospered under his administration . . . that he was rarely guilty of acts of atrocity, and that upon the whole he was admitted to be one of the mildest sovereigns that had ruled Siam'. Then, in a telling comment on the stability of Bangkok, he remarked that: 'the property of a merchant or stranger . . . is as secure from treachery or violence . . . as it would be in the best regulated city in Europe'.

Rama II died in 1824 at the age of 56 and is honoured today by Wat Amphawa Chetiyaram – built on the site of his birthplace in Samut Songkhram – and its adjoining memorial park. It is a tranquil spot, perhaps fittingly so for a monarch whose reign historians tend to view as an 'interlude'.

Taken gravely ill quite suddenly and losing the power of speech in his last days, Rama II died without designating an heir. It was left to the Accession Council, consisting of leading princes and high officials, to decide on a successor. Their choice was to offer the crown to Prince Chetsadabodin, who ascended the throne as King Phra Nangklao, Rama III (1824–1851). There has always been some debate about the merits of the succession, with some scholars arguing that while Chetsadabodin was Rama II's eldest surviving son, he was born to a concubine, whereas Prince Mongkut (who would later become King Mongkut, Rama IV), though his junior by some years, was the son of a queen of royal blood. The speculation, for what it is worth, is that shortly before his illness Rama II ordered Mongkut to enter the monkhood, ostensibly to counter the ill-omened death of a white elephant, but more likely, it has been suggested, to protect him from political intrigue, since Rama II knew that Chetsadabodin was a court favourite.

ABOVE

Phra Nangklao, King Rama III, a largely conservative monarch, a champion of Buddhism and Thai traditions, had to contend with regional conflicts throughout much of his reign, while relations with the West were becoming increasingly pressing.

As it was, the succession was untroubled and Rama III's first concern was with foreign relations. With matters mostly unresolved by the Crawfurd embassy in the previous reign, the British again sought a treaty with the Thais that would serve both diplomatic and commercial aims. The move was prompted by three main factors: one, Britain was at war with neighbouring Burma and was anxious that the Thais remain at least neutral; two, Britain wanted a settlement of the situation in the Malay states, which had been fractious since the 1821 Thai invasion of Kedah; and three, there was a desire for an easing of trade restrictions.

Instructed by the British Governor-General of India to secure these aims and maintain friendly relations with the Thais was Captain Henry Burney, a man with wide experience of the region. Arriving in Bangkok in late 1825, Burney initially made little headway, with the Thais deliberating amongst themselves; it was not until June 1826 that a treaty of friendship and commerce was signed. The main political agreement was on the acceptance of Thai influence in the Malay states of Kedah, Kelantan, Trengganu and Pattani, while Perak and

Selangor were to be independent. In terms of trade the Thais made tax concessions, and simplified a previously complicated system by replacing various fees imposed on shipping with a single duty according to the width of a ship's beam.

The treaty may not have been all that was desired – Rama III resisted granting any major trading advantages and, for example, the system of royal monopolies remained – but it did promote significant growth in Thai foreign trade with British territories.

Besides the British, the Americans were beginning to show interest in the kingdom. In 1833 President Andrew Jackson appointed the first US envoy to Bangkok, Edmund Roberts, who swiftly concluded a Treaty of Amity and Commerce. Its primary intention was to establish 'a perpetual Peace between the United States of America and the Magnificent Kingdom of Siam'. However, no significant trade concessions were offered, which dashed the expectations of US merchants, and it was the activities of US missionaries that were most visible at this time. In 1833 an American Baptist mission arrived in Bangkok and was shortly followed by a group of Presbyterians. The latter included Dr Dan Beach Bradley, who became a notable figure pioneering foreign medical aid and also, together with colleagues, setting up Bangkok's first printing press in 1835.

Western influence and international trade were now on the rise, although it was local problems that dominated much of the Third Reign and the Thais had to contend with troublesome vassal states in the east and south. The Lao forces under Chao Anu of Vientiane attacked in 1827, and took Nakhon Ratchasima and Saraburi before being defeated and repulsed. The war gave rise to another heroic episode, perhaps only a legend albeit one that is popularly believed, when the wife of the Deputy Governor of Nakhon Ratchasima, named Mo (subsequently given the title Thao Suranari), bravely rallied the people against their captors so that they liberated themselves. A memorial shrine in Nakhon Ratchasima was later built in Mo's honour and is still much revered.

Although the Lao had been defeated and Anu was captured in 1829 and taken to Bangkok, where he died, Rama III was determined to put a decisive end to rebellion. Save for its Buddhist temples, Vientiane was destroyed and the population was resettled west across the Mekong River in Thai territory. A policy of resettlement was continued over a number of years, resulting in part in the sizeable ethnic Lao population that characterizes large parts of north-east Thailand.

Rama III also had to contend with the rebellious southern vassal state of Kedah, which rose up in 1831 and again in 1839; only by the 1840s was the area settled, partly by a change in policy whereby Malay leaders were allowed to rule in place of Thai governors. As in the case of Laos, the outcome of the troubles in the south ultimately strengthened the position of the Thais.

A third area of hostility, and the most serious, was Cambodia, where Rama III engaged the Vietnamese in a series of campaigns that were part of the long-standing vying for supremacy in the Khmer lands. Warfare began in 1833 and continued for 14 years, with neither side able to sustain any lasting military victory. Eventually a stalemate was reached and both sides agreed to make peace, although the Thais could be seen to have won an advantage in that the agreement reached with the Vietnamese included a pro-Thai monarch being installed on the Cambodian throne in 1848.

TEMPLE ARCHITECTURE KING UNDER RAMA III

No outline of the Third Reign would be complete without some mention of the cultural accomplishments of the period. Rama III did not possess the literary talent of his father, nor did he seem to value the arts very highly, but he was a champion of Buddhism and Thai traditions. He was responsible for the building of three new temples and the restoration of 35 others, the hallmark of his architectural style being decoration with pieces of Chinese porcelain (as seen, for example, at Wat Arun).

More than simply adding to Thailand's religious architecture, Rama III had specific aims, which are clearly exemplified by two notable projects. One was the construction of the Phra Samut Chedi on what was then an island at the mouth of the Chao Phraya River (silting has since joined it to the riverbank). The purpose here was to announce to all arrivals that Thailand was a Buddhist kingdom, and it certainly had an impact. It remains today an attractive if obscure sight though to visitors by ship in the past it was inescapabley eye-catching. Anna Leonowens of *The King and I* fame wrote in her characteristic purple prose on her arrival in 1862 that:

It is perhaps the most unique and graceful object of architecture in Siam; shining like a jewel on the broad bosom of the river, fantastic and gilded, flashing back the glory of the sun, and duplicated in shifting shadows in the limpid waters below

The other major work was the restoration of Wat Pho (Wat Phra Chetuphon). This is Bangkok's oldest and largest temple, and had always served as a storehouse of traditional knowledge. Rama III enlarged on this. The superb 46-metre (150-foot) image of the Reclining Buddha, built in 1832, for which Wat Pho is most famous, was constructed as an act of merit making, but even more remarkable are Rama III's additions to the temple's role as a kind of university. He added masses of wall paintings, and inscribed stone slabs and statuary that record traditional knowledge and instruction on all manner of subjects, from astrology to medicine and massage. It was Rama III's aim that Wat Pho would preserve elements of Thai learning that might otherwise die out as the country modernized. The temple remains to this day the national centre for the preservation and teaching of traditional Thai medicine and massage.

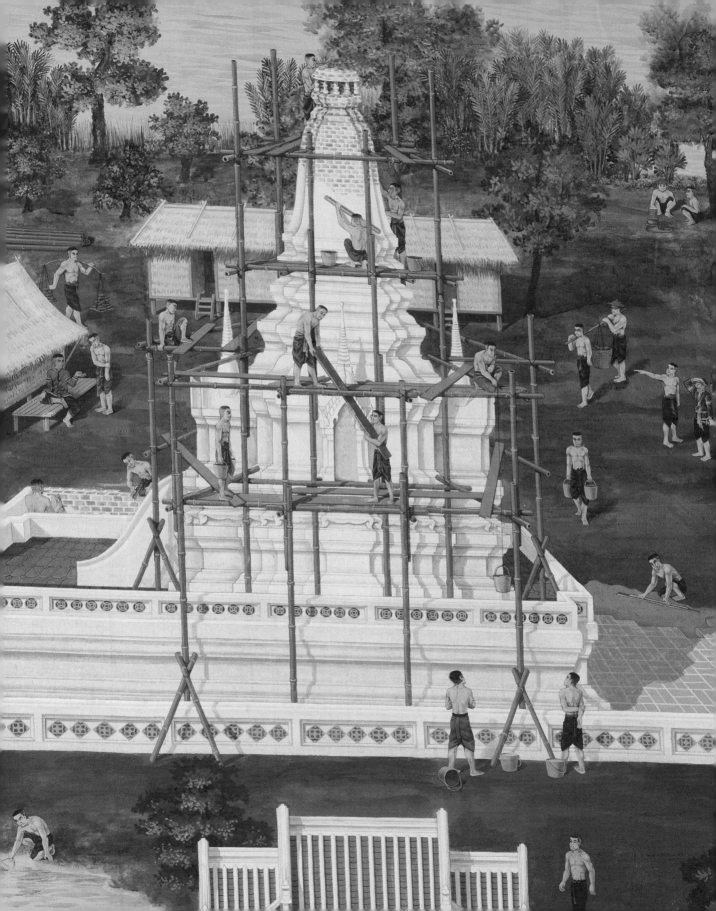

RIGHT

It was King Rama III's intention that the Phra Samut Chedi, being the first sight encountered by visitors arriving up the Chao Phraya River, would announce the kingdom as a Buddhist land.

OPPOSITE

In his restoration of Bangkok's Wat Pho King Rama III included wall paintings, engravings and statuary recording details of medicine, massage and other subjects of ancient learning.

The huge Reclining Buddha, 46 metres (151 feet) long, was commissioned by King Rama III as part of his restoration of Wat Pho, the temple that he intended should preserve traditional Thai knowledge and instruction.

If Rama III's accomplishments are indicative of what scholars view as a conservative period, events at the close of the Third Reign pointed towards the challenges of the future and the radical changes that would be needed if the Thais were to avoid dangers that threatened their independence. In 1850 Britain and the US separately sent missions to Bangkok to demand far greater trade concessions and diplomatic status than had earlier been won (in particular extra-territorial rights such as those that the British had secured for themselves in China after the Opium War of 1839–1842). Both envoys failed to achieve anything, mainly because Rama III was ailing and the court was preoccupied with the question of succession, although this did not lessen the envoys' anger and resentment at what they saw as Thai reluctance to negotiate.

MODERNIZATION AND WESTERNIZATION: 1851–1910

A few weeks before his death on 3 April 1851, Rama III made it known that he would not name a successor. The decision was left to a council of leading princes and officials which, influenced by prominent nobles, offered the throne to Mongkut, Rama III's half-brother, who had stayed in the monkhood throughout the Third Reign. Aged 47, Mongkut accepted and took the name Phra Chomklao, although he remained most widely recognized as King Mongkut, Rama IV (1851–1868).

Mongkut is known to the West through the Rodgers and Hammerstein musical and Hollywood films *The King and I*, based on Margaret Landon's novel *Anna and the King of Siam*, which in turn was inspired by two volumes of memoires by Anna Leonowens, one-time English governess to the monarch's children. This is unfortunate as the dramatic productions are a travesty of history, painting an entirely false picture of Mongkut (the films are banned in Thailand as being disrespectful to the monarchy), and clouding a proper appraisal of a remarkable man who came to the fore at a remarkable period in Thai history.

At the time of Mongkut's accession Thailand was threatened by Western imperialism, particularly by Britain and France which, during the latter half of the 19th century, established a stranglehold on the region. Britain secured colonial possessions in Burma to the west and the Malay states to the south, while France took control of the Indochinese peninsula in the east. Eventually only Thailand was to maintain its independence, and how it succeeded in doing so was in large part due to the enlightened thinking and astute policies of Mongkut.

OPPOSITE

A portrait of Anna Leonowens, English governess to King Mongkut's children made famous as the 'I' of The King and I *musical and film.*

BELOW

A group photo in front of the original offices of the Louis T. Leonowens Company, a trading firm established by Anna's son in 1905 that was to have lasting success.

RIGHT

King Mongkut, Rama IV, was the first monarch of the Chakri dynasty to take an outward-looking stance, seeking both to learn from the West and to protect his kingdom from Western imperialism.

KING MONGKUT – AN ENLIGHTENED RULER

Mongkut brought something new to the Thai monarchy; he was outward looking, hungry for knowledge and receptive to ideas from the wider world. Above all, he was prepared for change that would both foster the development of Siam and protect it from external threats.

For 27 years before becoming king Mongkut had been a Buddhist monk. During that time he immersed himself in Buddhist and Pali studies, and in 1833 founded the Thammayut Nikaya, a reformed order of monks, which followed, he believed, most closely the orthodoxy of the Theravada school. The sect, centred on Bangkok's Wat Bowonniwet, of which Mongkut became abbot in 1836, is today one of the two principal denominations of Buddhism in Thailand.

In parallel with distinguishing himself as a Buddhist scholar, Mongkut actively pursued Western knowledge, befriending American and French missionaries, notable among them being French Catholic Bishop Pallegoix. He learned Latin and English, and a proficiency in the latter opened the way to his reading widely on a variety of subjects, including science, mathematics, geography, history and astronomy. He took an enquiring and rationalistic approach to his studies and was not uncritical, reputedly famously commenting on the missionaries' Christian doctrine as 'What you teach people to do is admirable, but what you teach them to believe is foolish.'

Thus Mongkut ascended the throne not, as might be expected after his years in the monkhood, as an unworldly man, but as someone with a keen intellect and a broad understanding of the world fostered by friendship and dialogue with Westerners Such a combination of personal attributes was to prove vital in guiding the nation.

Mongkut was initially confronted by the age-old problem of regional warfare, this time conflict between the Shan states of Keng Tung and Chiang Hung, with the latter having sought Thai support during the previous reign, when Rama III saw an opportunity to exert Thai control over the area. Mongkut followed up with two expeditions against Keng Tung, in 1852–1853 and 1854, although both failed mainly due to logistic problems and the campaign was halted.

Attention quickly turned to the more pressing question of relations with the West, especially with Britain. Mongkut was aware of British frustration over the failure of the mission in 1850, and early in his reign he had entered into correspondence with the British authorities in Singapore and Hong Kong. Finally both sides saw that the time was ripe for further negotiation and Sir John Bowring, Governor of Hong Kong, was sent as Queen Victoria's envoy to Bangkok. The outcome was the Bowring Treaty of 1855, the first of the historic agreements between Siam and the major Western powers that granted generous trade concessions, as well as extra-territorial rights. The lifting of the tariff and royal monopoly restrictions that Bowring secured heralded a new age of commerce and international relations. However, although the negotiations were

amicable, Britain backed its claims with a scarcely veiled threat of force should talks break down. It is difficult not to read Bowring's report on the conclusion of the treaty with a cynical eye. 'We took departure,' he wrote, 'from a country the recollections of which are associated in our minds with nothing but grateful recollections and hopeful anticipations.'

In what was an unequal treaty, the Thais were forced to bow to the economic and political clout of a Western power and abandon the non-liberal principles of their traditional Sino-centric commerce in favour of free trade. The concessions granted, especially the reduction of import taxes to 3 per cent, were a blow to the national treasury ('my success involved a total revolution in all the financial machinery of the [Thai] Government', Bowring recorded) while, on the other hand, they did result in the dramatic growth of the commercial sector as they opened up foreign trade to ordinary people for the first time.

Over the next decade treaties with similar concessions to the ones the British had been granted were signed with the US, France, Denmark, the Netherlands, Prussia, Belgium and Italy. Negotiations were for the most part smooth and friendly, although the American envoy Townsend Harris could not help recording in his journal, 'It is an old saying here (Bangkok) that those who come here for business should bring one ship loaded with patience, another loaded with presents, and a third ship for carrying away the cargo.'

Trade increased enormously in the wake of the foreign treaties. Its annual value, derived principally from vastly expanded rice exports, almost doubled between 1850 and 1868 and in the process transformed the economy and society of the fertile Central Plains. Commercial growth brought physical change to Bangkok with the development of godowns and wharfs along the port frontage of the Chao Phraya River and, most significant of all, the construction in 1864

of the city's first paved road built to be capable of taking wheeled traffic. Named 'New Road', this followed a former elephant path and ran, as it still does, from the royal city past Chinatown and on to what was to become Bangkok's foreign and commercial hub for the big European trading houses that were set up in the latter half of the 19th century.

Mongkut's aim in signing foreign treaties with various countries was not simply one of commercial interests; he was also anxious to avoid the dominance of any one nation and the possible danger inherent in bilateral agreements of succumbing to Western colonial designs. In so managing foreign relations, Mongkut displayed considerable diplomatic skill and an acute understanding of the power plays acted out by the various Western nations, especially the English and the French in, respectively, the Malay Peninsula and Cambodia, which posed real threats. In 1862 the British deployed a warship to counter Thai designs on Kuala Trengganu, and in the following year Cambodia, ostensibly under Thai suzerainty, agreed to become a French protectorate, a decision that the Thais had no alternative but to accept.

Culturally, Mongkut sought to sidestep any moral justification for imperialism by showing Siam as a 'civilized' kingdom. For example, he hired American and British missionaries to teach the English language at court, ordered the nobility to wear shirts on official occasions so that they would not appear 'barbaric' to Western eyes and abolished for all Westerners the custom of crawling before the king at royal audiences. Mongkut was also quick to appreciate technological advantages. While still in the monkhood, he saw the potential of the printing press set up by Dr Dan Beach Bradley in 1835, and later as king he started a government gazette.

Regarding internal reforms and innovations, Mongkut had of necessity to move cautiously. Small but significant changes included the setting up of a mint at the palace, which issued flat coins to replace the round lumps of gold and silver previously in circulation. Major reforms would wait until the next reign, but Mongkut laid the groundwork and established a climate of change in which those reforms could be made.

Mongkut died in October 1868 after contracting malaria while on a visit to Prachuap Khiri Khan province to witness a solar eclipse that he had correctly calculated. He had not named a successor, but had expected the Accession Council

OPPOSITE
Constructed in 1864, New Road, or Charoen Krung, was Bangkok's first paved road suitable for wheeled traffic. By the end of the century it was at the heart of the city's developing business and commercial district.

to select his eldest son by a queen, Prince Chulalongkorn, who in due course was unanimously chosen and crowned King Chulalongkorn, Rama V (1868–1910). His reign of 42 years was to be pivotal, including unprecedented change and reform that thoroughly modernized the kingdom as a nation state.

At the time of his accession Chulalongkorn was still a 15-year-old minor, and for five years Chao Phya Si Suriyawong, the most powerful government official at the time, acted as regent. Nonetheless, the young king had been well

groomed for his role. Under his father's direction he received both a classic Thai education and a thorough grounding in Western studies (Anna Leonowens was one of his tutors). Eager to learn more and see at first hand possible models for his country's development, he toured Singapore, Dutch-controlled Java and British India, before attaining his majority and being crowned king in his own right on 16 November 1873. The trip to Singapore and Java in 1871 was notable in that it was the first time a Thai monarch had left the kingdom since Naresuan went to war in Burma in the early 17th century.

ABOVE

King Chulalongkorn, pictured here in an informal photograph taken in France, made two royal state visits to Europe, in 1897 and 1907.

Immediately following this second coronation, Chulalongkorn embarked on initiating the first of a series of wide-reaching social, political and administrative reforms that came to characterize his reign. These were designed to modernize the state and to centralize authority in Bangkok, while also limiting the powers of the hereditary nobility. Notable among them was the creation in 1874 of the Council of State, a legislative body, and the Privy Council, a personal royal council based on the British model.

Opposition was quick to show itself. In 1874 some radical members of Chulalongkorn's Privy Council began to call for the king's right to choose his own successor, which was a direct attack on Prince Wichaichan, the 'Second King' who occupied the Front Palace and had been named heir presumptive by Chao Phya Si Suriyawong. Forces at both the main palace and the Front Palace were put on alert. Matters came to a head on the night of 28 December, when a fire broke out near the gunpowder storeroom in the main palace. Armed troops from the Front Palace arrived ostensibly to assist in putting out the fire, but were refused admittance. Fearing that the incident would be used against him, Prince Wichaichan took refuge in the British Consulate, but the British were of the view that this was a domestic affair and the 'Second King' was forced to accept a reduced role.

What has become known as the Front Palace Crisis was a dangerous moment and illustrated how the power of nobles and royal relatives constrained the monarchy. Chulalongkorn was thus further motivated to reform a political system that had changed hardly at all since the Ayutthaya era. However, he did learn the lesson that reforms would have to be gradual. As to the immediate cause of the opposition, the title of 'Second King', or 'King of the Front Palace', was later abolished and replaced by the Western-style title 'Crown Prince of Siam'.

LEFT
The royal inauguration of Chalermlok Bridge marking the 40th year of King Chulalongkorn's reign in 1908. During the reign it had become an almost annual custom to open a new public bridge on the monarch's anniversary.

BELOW
A postcard, with stamps, from the Rama V era promoting the Kingdom's postal service, which was one of several modern innovations that were introduced during the Fifth Reign.

THE POST IN SIAM.

KEY REFORMS UNDER KING CHULALONGKORN

With judicious manoeuvring, aided in time by the natural passing of the old guard, Chulalongkorn succeeded in bringing about radical change, frequently by appointing his very able brothers and other close relations to key positions. For example, Prince Thewawong, a brother of three of his queens, headed the Ministry of Foreign Affairs, and Prince Chakkraphat, a brother, was placed in charge of the Ministry of Finance. These and other ministries (12 in all) were founded by Chulalongkorn as part of his determination to radically overhaul and modernize the administrative system, doing away with the 'departments' that had existed since Ayutthaya times and replacing and expanding them along Western lines. In the process practices were likewise modernized and, for example, a complete remodelling of the judiciary system followed the creation of the Ministry of Justice in 1892.

Regarding social reforms (the idea of which Anna Leonowens is reputed to have instilled in the mind of her one-time pupil), Chulalongkorn is best known for abolishing slavery, the phasing out of which was begun in 1873 and completed by the early years of the 20th century. Also early in his reign, he did away with the practice of people having to crawl on their hands and knees in the presence of the king, thus extending to all what his father had granted to Westerners.

Chulalongkorn's son King Prajadhipok, Rama VII, once described his father's reforms as 'revolutionary'. This was not strictly the case as change was brought about from within a legitimate position of power, namely the throne, yet the scale and scope of the reforms during the course of the Fifth Reign were immense and had an impact on virtually all spheres of political, administrative and social life.

Efforts to modernize the army and navy initiated in the previous reign were continued, with the creation of the Chulachomklao Royal Military Academy in 1887 to train troops in Western fashion, and a conscription law introduced in 1905. Then, beginning in 1897, centralized authority was strengthened, with the provincial administration of the kingdom divided into *monton* (circle),

changwat (province) and smaller subdivisions, each with officials appointed by Bangkok to govern them. A few local rulers attempted resistance but were quickly suppressed, and the kingdom effectively became a nation state rather than a network of city-states as it had long been.

Essential to the success of administrative reforms was an education system to produce qualified officials. Traditionally, a somewhat narrow education was provided by Buddhist monasteries and it was Chulalongkorn, understanding the need for modern education, who initiated the first proper schools as such. In 1871 a school for princes and court officials was opened in the Grand Palace, but the landmark year was 1884, which saw the first state school for ordinary people open at Wat Mahannoppharam in Bangkok. Educational progress was sustained by the founding in 1885 of the Department of Education, later raised in status to become the Ministry of Public Instruction.

LEFT

Vimanmek Teak Mansion, reputed to be world's largest golden teakwood building, was originally constructed on the island of Ko Si Chang and was later moved to Bangkok to be included in the Dusit Palace complex. Today it is preserved as a museum with art objects and other exhibits from the Rama V era.

OPPOSITE

The emblem of Chulachomklao Royal Military Academy founded by King Rama V in 1887 to provide modern army training along Western lines. The motto reads 'Unity Brings Happiness'.

Modernization went hand in hand with westernization, and the Fifth Reign saw a taste for and a fascination with all things European. Chulalongkorn made two royal state visits to Europe, in 1897 and 1907, the first taking nine months and spanning 16 countries. Cordially welcomed and fêted by the Western monarchs and heads of state of the day, Chulalongkorn was successful in promoting relations between Thailand and the European powers, and in firmly placing his kingdom on the world map. Even before his royal tours Chulalongkorn followed Western influences in developing Bangkok and was inspired not only to modernize the city, but also to glorify it through monumental building that incorporated Western designs and technology.

Among the many striking buildings that resulted is the Chakri Maha Prasat Throne Hall at the Grand Palace. Built between 1876 and 1882, this imposing structure was designed by British architect John Clunish in what can be described loosely as Victorian Italianate style. The original plans called for the structure

ABOVE

A portrait of King Chulalongkorn featured as part of the architectural decoration adorning the Chakri Maha Prasat Throne Hall at the Grand Palace.

OPPOSITE

Designed by an English architect in Victorian Italianate style, the Chakri Maha Prasat Throne Hall is one of the most striking examples of the Western-influenced style that became popular during the Fifth Reign.

to be topped by three domes, but conservative elements at court thought this was going too far and persuaded King Chulalongkorn to replace the domes with Thai-style roof spires, so preserving some element of traditional palace design. Opinions differ as to the building's success, but 'however else it may be judged', writes Clarence Aasen in *Architecture of Siam*, 'it was clearly a strategically de-rived aesthetic that was applied; it was not simply an arbitrary or purely technical decision, but in a considered manner interpreted and gave form to the thinking and conditions of the time, local as well as international'.

The Chakri Maha Prasat Throne Hall and other architectural monuments in and around the Grand Palace do not present a complete picture of King Chulalongkorn's vision, which was given its fullest expression in Bangkok's Dusit area. Lying to the north-east of the Grand Palace, Dusit was planned as a new royal city, a garden city, spacious and majestic with residences for the king and his family laid out in landscaped grounds. To connect this new royal city to the Grand Palace, King Chulalongkorn commissioned the construction of Ratchadamnoen Avenue, based partly on the Champs Elysées in Paris and partly

on The Mall in London. It retains its grand proportions although its look has been spoiled by the rather severe architectural style of buildings put up in the 1930s and '40s.

Fascination with the West was not all about style and during Chulalongkorn's reign the amenities of Bangkok were greatly improved. More roads and bridges were built and it became something of a tradition that a new bridge for public use was opened almost every year on the anniversary of the king's birthday. An increase in wheeled traffic followed, with trams being introduced in 1888 (at first horse drawn and later converted to electricity). The first car appeared on the roads in 1902, the vehicle belonging to Prince Rabi, one of Chulalongkorn's elder sons. Railways were constructed under a concession awarded to a Belgian-Danish company, with the first train service, a 25-kilometre (15½–mile) link

THIS PAGE
Following the opening of the first railway line in 1893 and the first car appearing on the roads in 1902, transportation developed rapidly in the early years of the 20th century.

OPPOSITE
A modern view of Ratchadamnoen Nok Avenue leading to the Ananta Samakhom Throne Hall at the heart of the Dusit area, focus of Bangkok's development during the Fifth Reign.

between Bangkok and today's Samut Prakan, opening in 1893. Other innovations of the age included the telephone, a parcel-post service and electric lighting.

Along with the changing face of Bangkok was a population that was increasingly cosmopolitan, as more and more Westerners were brought to the capital for employment by the big trading houses and the Crown, the latter having at the time some 200 foreign advisers and experts in fields such as engineering, mining, surveying and finance. Outstanding among the foreigners in royal service was Gustave Rolin-Jaequemyns, an international lawyer and formerly Belgium's interior minister who Chulalongkorn engaged as his general adviser in 1892. Ill health and old age led to his retirement in 1899, but during his seven years in royal service he proved to be a remarkably able and loyal servant of the country, playing a major role in Chulalongkorn's programme of reforms, particularly in the legal sphere, where he elaborated a Provisional Code of Criminal Investigation, a Civil Procedure and a Law on Evidence.

Casting a shadow over the extraordinary achievements of the Fifth Reign was the threat of colonization, the kingdom being bordered by British and French colonial possessions that could easily exert pressure on Thai sovereignty. Britain was the less aggressive of the two and its basic policy was to leave Thailand as a buffer state, using diplomacy and conciliation to secure its interests. However, its important commercial activity of teak extraction in Burma had the potential to expand into northern Thailand. Chulalongkorn responded to this by measures to bring quasi-autonomous Chiang Mai more directly under the control of the central government, with the appointment of a royal commissioner in 1874.

The situation was different in the south, where Thai suzerainty over the Malay sultanate states of Kedah, Perlis, Kelantan and Trengganu came under increasing British pressure. After a long period of negotiations the Thais were forced to cede suzerainty to the British by the Anglo-Siamese Treaty of 1909. In spite of Britain agreeing in return to transfer its consular jurisdiction of its nationals in the kingdom to the Thai courts, the treaty was decidedly one-sided and was part of the price for preserving independence.

France proved much more of a threat to Thai sovereignty. With control of Vietnam and Cambodia under a protectorate, the French looked to acquire the territory that is today Laos, which at the time fell within Bangkok's sphere of influence. This was partly because they sought a 'river road' to China via the

Mekong River, which was explored by the Garnier Expedition of 1866–1868 (cataracts on the river were found to make the dream of a commercial trade route impracticable), and partly to match the imperial expansion of Britain in Burma.

LEFT
Foreign advisers and experts in diverse fields were increasingly taken into government service during the late 19th and early 20th centuries, the most illustrious among them being Gustave Rolin-Jaequemyns, who was appointed King Chulalongkorn's General Adviser in 1892.

CONFRONTATION WITH THE FRENCH

For some years France manoeuvred to establish a claim to Laos, for which its main agent was Auguste Pavie, a noted explorer with a great knowledge of the region and its people who was made French vice-consul in Luang Prabang in 1886 and later French resident minister in Bangkok. France justified its ambitions by claiming that as the 'protector' of the Vietnamese Empire its protectorate should also include Laos, over which Vietnam had suzerainty at one time. This, writes David K. Wyatt, was 'in defiance of historical reality', and 'manufactured for the purpose of imperial aggrandizement'.

Rising tensions culminated in early 1893, when a French officer commanding troops sent to occupy Lao territory was shot and killed by the officer in charge of the defending Thai forces, Phra Yot Mueang Khwan. France saw this as a justification for war and sent gunboats to blockade the Chao Phraya River. In defiance of orders from Paris not to enter the river, the gunboats proceeded to Paknam, at the mouth of the river, resulting in a short engagement with Thai shore batteries – an event popularly known as the 'Paknam Incident'.

A witness to the confrontation, H. Warrington Smyth, the British director of mines, bluntly pointed out the dilemma in which the Thais found themselves. 'I doubt if those responsible for the defences,' he wrote, 'ever considered what would happen if they succeeded in sinking a French ship. The whole French nation would have risen with a shout, and vengeance could not have stopped short of the conquest of the country.'

Faced with an impossible situation, Thai Foreign Minister Prince Devawongse, in a display of characteristic diplomatic brilliance, congratulated the French commander on his success in getting past the Paknam forts and agreed to an immediate withdrawal of Thai troops from the east bank of the Mekong. France, however, pushed home its advantage to the hilt, with Pavie demanding the cession of the whole of Laos east of the Mekong. The Thais had little option but to accept and signed a Franco-Thai treaty in October 1893, the provisions of which also included the payment of three million francs in compensation, and punishment of the Thai officer Phra Yot Mueang Khwan. The trial of Phra Yot, whose defence rested on the claim that the French had opened fire first, resulted in his being found not guilty. This did not satisfy the French, who forced a second trial, held at the French Legation with a mixed court of three French and two Thai judges, that brought in a guilty verdict. Phra Yot was sentenced to 20 years imprisonment, although – hailed as a national hero – he served only four years before being granted a pardon.

It is an indication of the success of the massive reforms made during the Fifth Reign that while territorial concessions were made to France and Britain, they were effectively concluded with international recognition of the Kingdom's strength and integrity.

There is a certain paradox in that Chulalongkorn's reforms were made – indeed, arguably could only have been made – under an absolute monarchy, and yet such were the long-term results that W. A. Graham could claim in his 1924 book *Siam* that:

By these measures [reforms, particularly the abolition of corvee and the introduction of a poll tax paid in currency] the social conditions of lower class

OPPOSITE
The Mekong River forms the present-day border between Thailand and Laos, but in the 19th century Bangkok laid claim to the land on the river's eastern bank, a claim that was successfully challenged by the French.

life have been totally changed, so that instead of a servile and pauperized peasantry whose faces were for ever being ground, there is now growing up a sturdy and independent class free from the ancient thralldom, owning its own land, depositing money in the savings banks, in fact, acquiring a stake in the country and giving every evidence of the beginnings of coherent thought of its own.

Some might say that Graham overstated his case and that Thailand was not yet a modern nation, yet nonetheless it was moving rapidly and assuredly to becoming one.

NATIONALISM AND REVOLUTION: 1910–1934

King Chulalongkorn's death on 23 October 1910 was met with great public grief and mourning for the monarch who was to be remembered as Phra Piya Maharat, 'The Great Beloved King'. The anniversary of his death was later declared a national holiday in deference to his memory, and every year floral tributes are paid to his equestrian statue in Bangkok's Royal Plaza. Indeed, in Thai popular consciousness Chulalongkorn is held in reverence and respect that border on the mystical.

In accordance with Chulalongkorn's introduction of a new succession title, Prince Vajiravudh had been proclaimed Crown Prince in 1895. On the passing of his father he was duly crowned King Vajiravudh, Rama VI (1910–1925), initially at a small ceremony on 11 November 1910, and a year later in a much more lavish affair attended – for the first time at a Thai coronation – by representatives of foreign heads of state. He was well prepared to take on the duties of a monarch. He was highly educated and was the first Thai king to study overseas, in Britain, firstly with a private tutor, then at Sandhurst Royal Military Academy and later at Oxford University, where he read law and history. He was also versed in matters of state, having acted as regent during Chulalongkorn's second European tour in 1907.

Shortly after his coronation Vajiravudh declared in a speech that: 'I wish no honour greater than that of being my father's son who, having inherited the throne, walks in his footsteps in order to help complete the tasks necessary for the progress of the country.'

OPPOSITE

A gun emplacement at the mouth of the Chao Phraya that briefly saw action when the French sent gunboats to blockade the river in what became known as the 'Paknam Incident' of 1893.

ABOVE

The coronation parade of King Vajiravudh, Rama VI, on 11 November 1910, the first of two celebrations of the monarch's accession to the throne.

LEFT

For the first time at a royal Thai ceremony, representatives of foreign heads of state attended King Rama VI's much more lavish second coronation, which was held in 1911.

OPPOSITE

Coronation portrait of King Rama VI in full royal regalia.

ABOVE

Stamps of the Sixth Reign, one featuring the equestrian statue of King Chulalongkorn, the other a likeness of King Rama VI, while coins of the era have the monarch's image on the obverse side and a picture of the three-headed elephant Erawan on the reverse side.

ABOVE RIGHT

King Rama VI's love of the theatre is underscored in this postcard of the period showing an actress adorned in an elaborate theatrical costume.

Certainly, much of Vajiravudh's rule did provide continuity with the past and, most importantly, he succeeded in signing new treaties with the Western powers. Ever since the Bowring Treaty of 1855 and the others that followed shortly afterwards, the unfairness of the terms had rankled, especially the tariff privileges and extra-territorial rights they granted. Chulalongkorn had initiated moves to revise the treaties, but he died before he could accomplish his aims. It was Vajiravudh, through his Foreign Minister Prince Thewawong and, after his death in 1923, his son and successor Prince Devawongse Warothai, who finally managed to conclude what had been difficult and protracted negotiations.

The US was the first to sign a new treaty in 1920, with France and Britain following suit in 1925 and other powers shortly afterwards. The two most important provisions of these new agreements were Thai control of tariffs and the revision of extra-territorial rights. In other ways, too, Vajiravudh furthered the aims and policies begun by Chulalongkorn. There was ongoing improvement in the country's administration – for example, the Ministry of Local Government was combined with the Ministry of Interior, the Ministry of the Privy Seal was revived and the former Ministry of Public Works was changed to the Ministry of Communications. Similarly, modern education at all levels continued to be developed; Chulalongkorn University, the first Thai university, named in honour of King Chulalongkorn, was founded in 1917, while 1921 saw the enactment of the Primary Education Act of 1921, which enforced compulsory education for children aged 7–14 years.

BELOW

An early photograph of Chulalongkorn University, founded in 1917 as the country's first institute of higher learning and named in honour of Rama VI's father.

DEVELOPMENT OF TRANSPORT

Nowhere was the pace of modernization more apparent than in transportation. In 1914 construction of a southern railway line was begun, a development that incidentally gave rise to the country's first beach resort at Hua Hin, where the railway engineers built a halt. This coastal area on the eastern shores of the upper peninsula was gaining popularity among royalty and nobility as a summer retreat, and the coming of the railway made it so much more accessible. King Vajiravudh had a beachfront teakwood mansion built near Hua Hin in 1921, while the State Railway Department opened a resort hotel in 1923 which, renovated and expanded, remains today.

Even more significant than the expansion of the railways was the dawn of the aviation era. On 31 January 1911, Thais had their first glimpse of an aircraft when Belgian pilot Charles Van den Born brought his Henri Farman biplane for a week-long aviation meeting at the Royal Bangkok Sports Club, an event visited by Vajiravudh together with Prince Chakrabongse, Thai Army Chief of Staff, and Prince Purachatra, Commander of the Army Engineers. This directly prompted the formation of an army aviation unit, and three officers were sent to France to attend a flying course in early 1912. Two years later construction of Bangkok's Don Mueang Airport was undertaken. Its completion in 1915 marked the beginning of military and civil aviation in the kingdom.

RIGHT

The former Railway Hotel opened in the resort of Hua Hin in 1923 is today reincarnated as the Centara Grand Beach Resort and Villas, although its expansion and renovation have remained largely faithful to the original colonial-style architecture.

As much as modernization was the theme of Chulalongkorn's reign and was continued by his successor, Vajiravudh's rule was more markedly characterized by royal patronage of nationalism. This largely sprang from his personal conviction, boosted by what he had learned and seen in his time spent overseas, although it was perhaps reinforced by a potential threat faced early in the reign. In February 1912 Vajiravudh learned of a plot to overthrow the government that was being hatched by a group of young army and navy officers. They were not unanimous in their aims and a common agreement on the need for a constitution was clouded by other motives. Not least of these was personal animosity towards Vajiravudh himself, prompted by his lavish spending and the time he devoted to what they saw as trivial literary pursuits. What was a fuzzy plan was easily nipped in the bud. Several arrests were made, although Vajiravudh showed clemency and the ringleaders were sentenced to 20 years' imprisonment rather than receiving the death penalty. In spite of its failure, the event nonetheless strengthened the king's resolve to assert his rule and secure his notion of the Thai nation, united under an identity that was both felt by the people and readily recognizable to foreigners.

Vajiravudh's first step to promote nationalism was his creation in 1911 of the 'Wild Tiger Corps', named after King Naresuan's Wild Tiger and Peeping Cats guerillas. It was patterned along the lines of Britain's Territorial Army, though while the latter came under the War Office and its units formed parts of regular regiments, the Wild Tiger Corps was independent of the Ministry of Defence and came under the king's direct command. In addition to being designed as a supplement to the regular army, the Corps was also intended to stimulate national unity by recruiting civil servants with a duty to defend 'nation, religion and monarchy' (Vajiravudh was the first to emphasize this trinity), and thus break down the confining personal and departmental interests of bureaucracy – 'the cultivation of mutual friendship', as he described it.

In spite of much time spent on parades and manoeuvres the Wild Tiger Corps was a failure, lapsing into more of an elitist clique than a nationalizing force. It was disbanded later in the reign, although its junior branch, the Boy Scout movement, continued. Other examples of Vajiravudh's efforts to strengthen nationalism, however, were more lasting. They included changing the design of the national flag from a white elephant on a red background to the present tricolour; creating the first national holidays (initially two, King Chulalongkorn

Memorial Day on 23 October, and Chakri Day on 6 April to commemorate the founding of the dynasty); encouraging football and other team sports; enacting a law requiring all families to have surnames, and encouraging a higher social status for women.

Vajiravudh further used his great passion for art and literature to express his ideas of community and civic pride. He was an accomplished and prolific writer in a wide range of literary forms, as well as a translator into Thai of various authors and dramatists, Shakespeare among them. With his love of theatre, Vajiravudh even went as far as to construct an entire model city, which he named *Dusit Thani* ('Town in Heaven'), where he demonstrated with friends and officials how an ideal liberal society would be run, although this was seen by most as mere play-acting.

In July 1917, after initially remaining neutral, Vajiravudh took the kingdom into the First World War on the side of the Allied Powers, believing that, as he said, 'this is an excellent opportunity for us to gain equality with other nations'. An expeditionary force of 1,200 volunteers was despatched to Europe. While the Thai volunteers arrived too late to see action, Thai troops did participate in the victory march in Paris on 19 July 1918, and overall Vajiravudh's display of support served to enhance Thai nationalism. Most significantly, it proved instrumental in facilitating the later favourable renegotiations of commercial treaties with Western countries.

Vajiravudh's reign was not a popular one, and it is viewed as controversial and even paradoxical. Although Vajiravudh was in many ways a genuine liberal and modernizer with his own idea of nationalism, he did not envisage any significant change of institutions. As historians Baker and Pasuk have astutely pointed out, Vajiravudh's vaunted trinity of 'nation, religion and monarchy' was in fact three parts that were the same rather than different, the king being 'the political embodiment of a nation of Buddhists, and the protector of both nation and religion'. Thus 'the phrase wrapped up a very traditional concept of royal power in the modern language of the nation'. Moreover the promotion of nationalism had the regrettable effect of stirring up anti-Chinese sentiment, fuelled especially by resentment of the dominant entrepreneurial role of the Chinese in the nation's economy – Vajiravudh used the term 'The Jews of the East' as the title of one especially hostile essay.

Overshadowing everything else in the last years of the reign was a financial crisis that threatened the country's stability. There were multiple causes for this, both internal and external. They included a rice shortage caused by drought in 1919, a foreign exchange crisis resulting from the rise in the price of silver after the First World War and, by no means least, Vajiravudh's own personal extravagance and costly expenditure on such unproductive projects as the Wild Tiger Corps. Attempts to redress matters and control public spending achieved little else than to stave off immediate disaster.

King Vajiravudh died on 26 November 1925. His only child, born just two days before his death, was a daughter. The crown passed, as he had wished in a letter, to his eldest surviving 'true' brother (that is, not a half-brother), Prince Prajadhipok, who became King Phra Pokklao (Prajadhipok), Rama VII (1925–1935).

Prajadhipok had not expected to ascend the throne. Vajiravudh was only 44 years old when he died, while Prajadhipok's other brothers, who were heirs apparent, had predeceased him. Although well educated in England at Eton and the Royal Military Academy at Woolwich, the 32-year-old monarch was otherwise ill prepared for government. Moreover the government he inherited was a

shambles, plagued by enormous financial problems and with no one seemingly agreeing on how to put matters right.

Prajadhipok quickly took what he hoped would be corrective measures and created a new advisory body, the Supreme Council of State, comprising talented and experienced men such as Prince Damrong Rajanubhab, the long-serving Interior Minister who had been one of King Chulalongkorn's close advisors. He also appointed new ministers, replacing all but three of Vajiravudh's cronies. These moves were designed to restore public confidence in the monarchy and the government and were partially successful, but they could scarcely secure a long-term solution. With Vajiravudh's reign widely blamed for the nation's financial problems, the new appointments of mostly senior members of the royal family, regardless of how capable and well intentioned they were, did not dispel popular fears of an elitist rule.

The question of political development had been in the air for some time. Both Chulalongkorn and Vajiravudh had considered ways of creating a more liberal government, although both had felt that a constitution was unsuited to Thai society. Prajadhipok likewise queried whether or not a representative government, perhaps similar to the British parliamentary system, would be appropriate or even workable, but none of his advisors encouraged such thinking. Nevertheless, the idea continued to dog him and he showed considerable understanding of the dilemma. In a 1927 memorandum he wrote: 'If it is admitted that some day we may be forced to have some form of democracy in Siam, we must prepare ourselves for it gradually. We must learn and we must educate ourselves.'

In retrospect, most would agree that Prajadhipok was correct in his argument for gradual change. However, events dictated otherwise. Efforts to cut government spending had some initial impact, only to be ultimately doomed by the Great Depression. This financial crisis of the American and European markets shocked Thailand in the early 1930s, most noticeably because of the plummeting price of rice, the mainstay of the country's economy.

Paralleling the fluctuation of economic fortunes was growing political criticism. This was fermented mainly by young military officers and students, predominantly law students pursuing their studies overseas. In the 1920s Bangkok's law school was the centre of advanced thinking, and it was from here that many students won scholarships to further their studies abroad. Most went to England, but several

LEFT
HRH Prince Damrong Rajanubhab (1862-1943), a half-brother of King Chulalongkorn, was one of several close relatives appointed by the monarch to key ministerial positions. In an eminent career, his talent and long experience were later called upon by King Prajadhipok during the last years of absolute monarchy.

opted for France and it was the latter who tended to be the more radical, fervently discussing amongst themselves ideas of socialism and popular democracy, although a desire for regime change arose more directly as a response to the global slump and retrenchment measures.

The most prominent of these students was a young lawyer named Pridi Phanomyong, who headed a secret association know as the 'Promoters of Political Change', later to become the People's Party, and a military cadet, Luang (Plaek) Phibun Songkhram. The revolutionary political ardour of these two, dubbed by their friends as, respectively, 'The Professor' and 'The Captain', did not diminish on their return to Bangkok and they continued to plot the overthrow of the government. By 1932 conditions were such that they were in a position to successfully stage a coup that changed Thailand's political system from an absolute monarchy to a constitutional monarchy. In the words of writer Alec Waugh: 'No revolution in the turgid history of mankind has been carried through so swiftly, so efficiently and so pacifically.'

THE 'PROMOTERS OF POLITICAL CHANGE'

THE PROFESSOR Pridi Phanomyong, known as 'The Professor' among the revolutionaries who were behind the coup of 1932, was a child prodigy. Born the son of a rice merchant in a village near Ayutthaya, he finished the prestigious Suan Kulab College and entered the Ministry of Justice's law school at the age of just 17. He was called to the bar two years later. In 1919 he tried and won his first and only court case as a defence lawyer, that of an elderly Chinese merchant held liable by the Crown for damages to royal property during a boating incident on the Chao Phraya River. By the age of 19 Pridi had already earned a reputation for legal and rhetorical skills. After further studies in Paris he returned to Bangkok in 1927 and was assigned to the Ministry of Justice's secretariat, where he acquired extensive knowledge in the drafting of laws. He also wrote a compilation of Thai laws from antiquity to modern times, which was published in several volumes.

THE CAPTAIN Like his revolutionary confrère Pridi, Luang Phibun Songkhram was a commoner, his parents owning fruit orchards just outside Bangkok. After his death his widow emphasized this background to put into focus Phibun's early achievements. He had taken first-place honours at the Cadet School and won a King's Scholarship to study in France. This was the more remarkable because, his widow wrote, 'in that period few commoners indeed could afford the expenses of sending their children to study abroad, and a very limited number of scholarships were available to their likes'. Although he was dubbed 'The Captain' by his revolutionary friends, Phibun was not just a simple soldier; he had a scholarly disposition and became a noted teacher of and writer on military science.

Virtually bloodless – there was only one casualty, a non-fatal shooting – the Revolution of 1932 (or 'coup' as some historians prefer) occurred on 24 June. At dawn a group of conspirators, self-styled 'Promoters', comprising 49 military officers and 65 civilians organized by Pridi Phanomyong and Luang Phibun Songkhram, succeeded mainly by surprise and bluff in occupying the Ananta Samakhom Throne Hall in Bangkok and taking hostage leading officials, mostly princes. Prajadhipok was staying at Klaikangwon Palace (translating as, ironically in the circumstances, 'Far From Worries') in Hua Hin. Here he received a letter from the conspirators demanding that he return to the capital to reign as king under a constitutional monarchy as established by their self-proclaimed People's Party (*Khana Ratsadorn*). He accepted what was a fait accompli and replied:

> I have received the letter in which you invite me to return to Bangkok as a constitutional monarch. For the sake of peace; and in order to save useless bloodshed; to avoid confusion and loss to the country; and, more, because I have already considered making this change myself, I am willing to cooperate in the establishment of a constitution under which I am willing to serve.

A provisional constitution accordingly came into effect on 27 June, followed by a permanent one on 10 December, a date that is still recognized in the Thai calendar by a national holiday. As summarized in the 1934 *Commercial Directory for Siam*:

> Under the New Constitution the Sovereign power emanates from the Siamese nation. The King, who is the head of the nation, exercises the legislative power by and with the consent of the Assembly of the People's Representatives, the executive power through the State Council and judicial power through the Courts duly established by law.

Fundamental though the change was, laying the foundations of the modern state, the coup of 1932 had little impact on daily life. The executive powers that had previously been held by princes were transferred to military men and bureaucrats, but as far as the ordinary citizen was concerned the monarch remained the ultimate figure of respect in what was and remains deeply rooted veneration.

The new government's first prime minister, Phraya Manopakonnithithada (Mano), was not one of the Promoters and had been president of the Supreme Appeal Court. Other ministers were also senior figures who had served in previous governments under the absolute monarchy. Presumably this was intended to help secure stability through experienced hands, although many minsters without portfolio were of the Promoters, Pridi Phanomyong and Lieutenant Colonel Plaek Phibun Songkhram among them. Given such a heterogeneous group, military and civilian, conservative and liberal, senior and junior, it is not surprising that rifts in the Cabinet soon appeared. The crunch came in early 1933, when the Assembly asked Pridi to draw up an economic plan and he duly presented a socialistic programme that, among other proposals, called for the nationalization of agricultural land. The majority was outraged, damning the plan as communistic. Following some near-violent scenes in the Assembly, Pridi was prompted by friends to resign and to slip quietly away into temporary exile in France.

In June of the same year Phraya Manopakonnithithada's government ended in a bloodless coup led by Colonel Phraya Phahon Phonphayuhasena, assisted by Luang Phibun Songkhram, who then held the rank of lieutenant-colonel, with the former becoming prime minister. Such continued bickering and mixed motives among the People's Party in only its first year in power disgruntled many, King Prajadhipok included, and in October 1933 Prince Boworadet, a former Minister of Defence, mounted an armed rebellion against the government. Having gained the support of garrisons in Nakhon Ratchasima, Saraburi and Ayutthaya, Boworadet headed towards Bangkok and took Don Mueang Airport, demanding the resignation of the government for its disrespect of the king and what he saw as its communist leanings. However, he failed to win over troops in the capital and was confronted by government forces led by Lieutenant-Colonel Luang Phibun. Virtual civil war broke out between 13 and 16 October, and only after fierce and bloody fighting were the rebels defeated, Boworadet managing to escape into exile in French Indochina.

The outcome of the insurrection was a strengthened government, a rise in Luang Phibun's popularity and a decline in Prajadhipok's standing even though he had not, as far as is known, supported the rebellion. Relations between the king and the People's Party continued to deteriorate. The king's principal concern, apart from losing certain royal prerogatives, was that he believed the

RIGHT
King Ananda, Rama VIII, was only 10 years old when he succeeded to the throne in 1935 and a Council of Regency was appointed while he completed his education in Switzerland, not returning to Thailand until after the end of the Second World War.

Assembly was becoming increasingly undemocratic. On 14 October 1934, while in Britain to receive medical treatment, Prajadhipok announced his intention to abdicate unless the government agreed to certain requests, one of which was that the constitution be amended to make the Assembly an entirely elected body. The government rejected the ultimatum and on 2 March 1935 the king abdicated, saying in a public message:

> I am willing to surrender the powers I formerly exercised to the people as a whole, but I am not willing to turn them over to any individual or any group to use in an autocratic manner without heeding the voice of the people.

After centuries of living under an absolute monarch, Thai society as a whole must have experienced some sense of loss, the absence of a father figure, someone charged with championing its interests. A difficult period of adjustment followed, and this partly explains why there was no opposition to the People's Party, a party over which the military loomed.

REGENCY AND THE SECOND WORLD WAR: 1935–1945

Prajadhipok remained in Britain, where he died at the age of 48 on 30 May 1941. As he had no children and had not designated a successor, the National Assembly followed Vajiravudh's 1924 Law of Succession and elected his nephew, Prince Ananda, as the legal heir. The eldest son of Prince Mahidol, King Ananda, Rama VIII (1935–1946) was ten years old at the time of his succession and was living with his mother, brother and sister (his father had died in 1929 when Ananda was four years old) in Lausanne, Switzerland. The National Assembly therefore appointed a Council of Regency consisting of Colonel Prince Anuwat Chaturon, Lieutenant Commander Prince Athit Thip-apha and an ennobled commoner, Chao Phraya Yommarat, a former Minister of the Interior.

Apart from a two-month visit in 1938–1939, Ananda was absent from the country for most of his short reign, completing his education overseas and returning only after the end of the Second World War. Meanwhile the broader changes initiated by the 1932 Revolution were taking effect, with growing popular involvement in politics. In spite of a government in the hands of an elite and beset by almost constant internal conflicts, important gains were made during

the 1930s. Public education, for example, was advanced with a considerably increased budget, and among other measures two notable schemes in 1932 and 1936 saw, respectively, the extension of primary education and a new emphasis on vocational training. Nationwide administration was also streamlined, while the economy was well if conservatively managed and showed good recovery from the Great Depression. The military budget was further boosted, which was partly self-serving given the sizeable military make-up of the government, but was also indicative of a genuine feeling among many of the need for security amid the probability of coming war.

In December 1938 Phraya Phahon Phonphayuhasena retired as prime minister and was replaced by Luang Phibun Songkhram, a man described by David

K. Wyatt as 'one of only a handful of people who definitively put their stamp on Thai history'. His first tenure, running from December 1938 to July 1944, was remarkable for its policy of mass nationalism put across to the public with the full effectiveness of propaganda methods modelled on those of authoritarian regimes in Europe. In a programme of national reconstruction aimed at making Thailand a progressive nation, Phibun exhorted the people to actively engage in change and embrace a new sense of nationhood through a set of cultural mandates, ranging from the requirement to salute the flag and know the national anthem, to the encouragement to work hard and the promotion of Western dress such as the wearing of shoes and hats. Patriotism was further spread through schools and in popular songs and dances.

Nationalism was most emphatically underscored by the change of the country's name from Siam to Thailand, *Prathet Thai*, in 1939. The word *prathet* translates as country, and although 'Thai' in this instance is often taken to mean 'free' – hence 'Land of the Free' – it was Phibun's intention that the name should reflect the country as belonging to the Thai people. This is fully stressed in the government's 'Thailand for the Thai' economic plan, which levied heavy taxes on foreign-owned companies, the majority of them Chinese, while providing government subsidies to Thai-owned business. The degree of antagonism towards the commercial dominance of the Chinese was made clear in 1938, when writer and propagandist Luang Wichitwathakan gave a public lecture in which he drew a parallel between the Chinese in Thailand and the Jews in Nazi Germany.

Phibun's nationalism was Western in inspiration (for example, 1 January was adopted as New Year's Day in place of the traditional Thai 1 April date), but not pro-Western. Rather, Phibun looked to Japan as the model of an Asian country that had achieved modernization using Western methods and technology, and sought to foster closer relations with the Japanese. Not all were as enthusiastic about this as Phibun, and Pridi (back in government after his self-imposed exile) along with several of the older conservative elements doubted the wisdom of the prime minister's foreign policy. Yet, it was Japan's support that aided the Thais when Phibun's nationalism reignited antagonism towards the French.

The humiliating events of 1893, when the French had used gunboat diplomacy to force Thailand to yield parts of Laos, had not been forgotten. In November 1940, with Indochina under the French Vichy government aligned with

OPPOSITE

With an obelisk and Western 'heroic' style statues, Victory Monument in Bangkok was erected in 1941 to commemorate the Franco-Thai Indochina conflict of November 1940–January 1941.

Germany, Phibun decided to invade the border areas of Laos and Cambodia in an attempt to regain lost territory. Sporadic fighting was ended in early 1941, when the Japanese stepped in and mediated a settlement whereby the Vichy French agreed to cede to Thailand 54,000 square kilometres (20,850 square miles) of Laotian territory west of the Mekong, and the Cambodian provinces of Battambang and Siem Reap. The episode is commemorated by the Victory Monument in Bangkok, an obelisk that is now at the centre of a congested traffic circle.

The success of this small-scale conflict hugely boosted Phibun's standing as a national leader, although this was soon overshadowed by Thailand's involvement in the Second World War. On 8 December 1941 Japan attacked the US naval base at Pearl Harbor, in Hawaii, so starting the war in East Asia. Previously, on 7 December, the Japanese ambassador to Thailand had called on Phibun to request the passage of Japanese troops through Thai territory to attack British Malaya, but the prime minister was away in the newly conquered territories in Cambodia, and in his absence Foreign Minister Direk Chaiyanam refused. It made no matter, because the next day Japan invaded Thailand at multiple points, with the strongest force being in the south around Songkhla and Nakhon Si Thammarat. Several hours of fighting were ended when Phibun, hastily called back to Bangkok, ordered a cease fire. While the Thais would have presumably preferred neutrality, it was obvious that resistance would be futile and there was therefore no alternative but to acquiesce to the Japanese in return for their recognition of Thailand's independence.

A month later, on 25 January 1942, Thailand declared war on Britain and the US. Quite why this was done is unclear; it was unnecessary and it can only be supposed that Phibun believed that the Japanese would win. As it was, not all were in agreement with the move and those who opposed it were forced out of government. They included Finance Minister Pridi, who was subsequently appointed to the non-political post of head of the Council of Regency.

War was not, however, ever officially declared against the US because the Thai ambassador in Washington, M. R. Seni Pramoj, refused to submit the document to the American government and instead set about forming a Free Thai (Seri Thai) movement, which received Allied support. Seni, a conservative aristocrat, had made his position clear from the start. In a statement to the US Department of State, dated 10 December 1941, he wrote:

A communique has just come through today from Bangkok to the effect that the Japanese armed forces have entered Thailand by land and sea . . . Under these circumstances it is no longer possible to be sure whether instructions reaching me from Bangkok are those of the Thai government or are dictated by the armed invaders . . . I therefore deem it my duty as the representative of my King, and of the free and independent Thailand which sent me here as its representative, to carry on the struggle for the freedom of Thailand . . . I have decided to work from now on for one thing and one thing only – the re-establishment of free and independent Thailand.

Although Japan stationed 150,000 troops in Thailand, the country was not occupied as such. British residents and other nationals of Allied countries were interned, but otherwise daily life was little affected. The main suffering caused by the war was brought about by Allied bombing raids and deteriorating economic conditions.

ABOVE
A parade of members of the Free Thai movement, which opposed the Japanese presence in Thailand during the Second World War and received the support of the Allies.

LEFT
Damage caused by Allied bombing raids and deteriorating economic conditions in Bangkok as the Second World War progressed eventually turned public opinion against Phibun Songkhram's pro-Japanese government.

DEATH RAILWAY

The single most tragic event of the Second World War in Thailand was the building of the infamous 'Death Railway'. As part of their war strategy to conquer Burma, the Japanese forced Allied prisoners of war, as well as Thai and other Asian labourers, to build a 415-kilometre (258-mile) railway between Thailand and Burma. A vital link in this supply line was a bridge to span the River Khwae Yai in Thailand's Kanchanaburi province. Engineers estimated that it would take five years to build the railway, but with construction commencing in September 1942, the Japanese army had it completed in 16 months at the cost of the lives of 16,000 British, Dutch, Australian, American, Malay and Indian PoWs, and an estimated 100,000 Thai and other Asian forced labourers, who died from inhumane treatment, malnutrition and disease.

After seeming unstoppable early in the war, Japan was losing ground by 1944 and its eventual defeat was becoming more and more apparent. At the same time, Free Thai agents, aided by the British Special Operations Executive and the US Office of Strategic Services, were successfully infiltrating the country. Eventually, rising casualties from Allied bombing and worsening economic hardship turned the public against Phibun, and in July 1944 he was ousted by the government, which was by now strongly influenced by members of the Free Thai movement. The National Assembly then appointed the liberal lawyer Khuang Aphaiwong as prime minister and Pridi as the sole regent in what was the first predominantly civilian government since 1932.

The war ended with Japan's surrender on 15 August 1945 and Allied military responsibility for Thailand fell to the British. Pridi as regent was swift in proclaiming that Thailand's declaration of war was null and void in that it was made contrary to the will of the people and in violation of the constitution. Because of his cordial if reluctant relations with the Japanese during the last year of the war, Khuang Aphaiwong felt it necessary to resign and was replaced briefly by Thawi Bunyaket before Seni Pramoj was invited to become the new prime minister.

Unlike the US, which had never officially been at war with Thailand, Britain, even though it had supported the Free Thai movement, did consider itself to have been at war with Phibun's government and sought onerous war reparations, including the right to station British and Commonwealth troops in the country. Weeks of tense negotiations with the Seni government were concluded only after the Americans persuaded Britain to reduce its demands, and an Anglo-Thai peace agreement was signed in January 1946. This marked the beginning of the end of British influence and the ascendancy of the US in Thailand as elsewhere in the non-communist world.

COUPS, CONSTITUTIONS AND THE STRUGGLE FOR DEMOCRACY: 1946–1980

International agreements after the Second World War were not matched by accord at home. The Seni government was not popular, due in part to inflation, reparation payments to Britain and the return of territory in the Shan States and Kayah State that Japan had allowed Phibun to annex. Moreover, as an aristocrat Seni was thought to be an elitist and out of touch with political realities. In order

BELOW
*Portrait in royal regalia of
His Majesty King Bhumibol
Adulyadej, Rama IX.*

to bring about greater political stability, Pridi, who was the real power with the majority support of the National Assembly, brought back Khuang Aphaiwong as prime minister in early 1946 before taking the post himself in March of that year. Pridi, who believed political strength lay in parliamentary politics, worked with his cabinet to draft a new constitution which, coming into effect in May 1946, called for a bicameral legislature with a House of Representatives elected entirely by popular vote and a Senate with members nominated by the lower house.

Elections held early in 1946, in which political parties participated for the first time, saw a coalition of Pridi's Constitutional Front and the Cooperative Party win a large majority of seats in the lower house, with Khuang Aphaiwong's Democrat Party and the Progressive Party of Kukrit Pramoj, brother of Seni, in opposition. For a moment it seemed as if a democratic civilian government would prosper, but expectations were soon shattered by tragedy.

On 9 June 1946 King Ananda, who had returned to Thailand six months earlier, was found shot dead in his bedroom in the Grand Palace. The mystery of the death has never been solved, remaining to this day a controversial and highly sensitive subject. The immediate outcome of the tragedy, however, was that public opinion turned against Pridi, who was seen as an anti-royalist, and held that the government was somehow responsible for Ananda's death. With rumours rife, Pridi resigned in August on the grounds of ill health and left the country. The late king's younger brother, 19-year-old Bhumibol Adulyadej, was chosen to succeed as King Rama IX (1946–2016). Born in the US and brought up in Switzerland, the new king had gone to Thailand for the first time in 1945 with his brother, and shortly after his succession he returned to Switzerland to complete his education, not returning until 1950.

Meanwhile the government stumbled on, but was unable to steady itself and was overthrown on 8 November 1947 by a military coup engineered by

Phibun. In spite of having been arrested as a war criminal after the Second World War but released by the courts shortly afterwards, Phibun had retained his constituency of supporters in the military as well as among some of the civilian elite fearful about the rise of communism in neighbouring countries. However, concerned over possible international criticism of an army-led government, the coup leaders appointed Khuang Aphaiwong as prime minister yet again and kept the 1946 constitution. Then, in spite of (or because of) the Democrats faring better than Phibun's party in the January 1948 elections, military action was threatened. Khuang was forced to resign and Phibun took over as prime minister on 8 April 1948.

Phibun was in power for nearly a decade, the period coinciding with the start of the Cold War and with communist insurrections in north Vietnam and Malaya. These prompted the 'Domino Theory', whereby the West feared that if one Southeast Asian country fell to communism others would inevitably follow. With Phibun well known for his right-wing politics, one British Foreign Office official described Thailand under Phibun as 'an anti-communist oasis in the middle of Southeast Asia'. As already noted, it was the US and not Britain that was now the major influence in the region. The Phibun era witnessed the beginning of a long tradition of US support for Thai military regimes, and a special relationship that would culminate in the 1960s with the Thais allowing US Air Force bases on Thai soil during the Vietnam War.

Under Phibun Thailand became something of a protégé of the US and was the recipient of American economic and military aid which, along with rice and other commodity exports, as well as the beginnings of a small-scale manufacturing sector, accounted for a strengthened Thai economy. In turn Thailand made a significant contribution to the anti-communist efforts in the region; it was the first Asian country to send troops to join the UN forces fighting the Korean War, and in 1954 it became a member of the South East Asia Treaty Organization (SEATO), which the US supported.

On the home front Phibun's regime sought strength through the intimidation of all opposition. Political opponents were arrested and tried; some were executed while others never reached trial and were shot in extrajudicial killings by the police. Two coups by the navy to oust Phibun were attempted in 1949 and 1951, but both were violently suppressed with heavy casualties, while Phibun

General, later Field Marshal, Sarit Thanarat takes control of student demonstrators protesting the election methods of Prime Minister Phibun Songkhram in 1957.

was almost killed in the latter coup when the ship on which he was being held captive was bombed by the air force and he was forced to swim to safety. (The event has gone down in history as the 'Manhattan Coup', named after the ship on which the prime minister was first taken hostage.)

In terms of domestic policies, Phibun reverted to his nationalism of the late 1930s. He reinstated the name 'Thailand' (the immediate post-Second World War government had reverted to 'Siam' as a reaction against the nationalists), improved secondary education and resumed legislation to regulate Thai social behaviour. Harassment of the Chinese continued, the tendency being to regard them as not only disloyal but also as communist.

A new constitution – the so-called third permanent constitution – which had been promulgated in March 1949 and allowed for a Senate appointed by the king, was annulled in November 1951 in a 'silent' coup by the military group within the government on the stated grounds of rooting out ministers who held communist ideas. The 1932 arrangements were reverted to and thus the National Assembly ceased to be an elected body. Phibun continued as prime minister, although he had an arch rival in General Sarit Thanarat, who was an increasingly threatening and ambitious challenger.

Shortly after returning from visits to the US and Britain in 1955, Phibun decided to organize elections, which were held in February 1957 – he was either newly inspired by liberalism or wanted to shore up support against his rivals. The move backfired terribly. Phibun's party won only by massive corruption – Sarit described the elections as 'filthy' – and there was a popular outcry against the government. Phibun survived in government until 17 September 1957, when he was forced to resign following a bloodless coup led by Sarit and subsequently went into exile.

New elections were held in December without any party winning a majority, and Sarit organized a loose coalition under the banner of the National Socialist

Party. He did not immediately become prime minister due to ill health, and instead appointed his deputy in the armed forces, Thanom Kittikhachon. However, after receiving medical treatment in the US, he later took control with Thanom's consent and imposed military rule in October 1958, under what became known as the Revolutionary Party.

Sarit, now with the rank of Field Marshal, believed that fundamental political changes were needed, but unlike other Thai leaders he had been educated entirely in Thailand and was thus little influenced by exposure to foreign ideas and life outside of Thailand. His aim was to restore the prestige of the monarchy and establish a stable society based on orderliness and hierarchy. Military rule was seen as the best way to achieve this, as well as to combat communism.

As the leader of the Revolutionary Party, Sarit addressed King Bhumibol in an official note and pledged to uphold the constitutional monarchy system of government. The gracious reply, delivered by the King's Principal Private Secretary, stated in part:

> His Majesty the King has graciously observed that the Revolutionary Party's objective of protecting the people, safeguarding national welfare and interest and promoting the prosperity of the country is a noble one. Having set yourself a noble objective, you are expected to proceed with your work with loyalty and uprightness, placing the interest of the nation above all.

KING BHUMIBOL ADULYADEJ, RAMA IX

The longest reigning monarch in Thai history, King Bhumibol Adulyadej was also the longest reigning monarch in the world up to his death in October 2016. More significant than longevity, however, was the character of the reign. King Bhumibol had in many ways redefined the role of an enlightened constitutional monarch, giving it fresh relevance in the modern world, while at the same time winning the deep reverence and respect of his people. Throughout the decades he had been a stable presence in the often stormy political life of the nation.

After completing his introductory trips overseas in the 1960s, King Bhumibol never left the country and concentrated his efforts on the well-being of the Thai people. He travelled in all areas of Thailand, including the remotest places, talking to people in order to understand their ways of life and problems, and find ways to help them. He initiated more than 4,000 royal development projects, ranging from irrigation to drought and flood alleviation, and from crop substitution to public health. These efforts received widespread international recognition, including the UN's first Human Development Lifetime Achievement Award presented to His Majesty in 2006.

Their Majesties King Bhumibol Adulyadej, Rama IX, and Queen Sirikit pictured on the occasion of His Majesty's coronation on 5 May 1950.

In January 1960 Sarit declared an interim constitution that provided for an assembly to draw up a new constitution – the eighth since 1932 – and although he assumed the office of prime minister, his regime was that of a military dictatorship. His government did, however, achieve the goals of political stability and economic growth. Indeed, Thailand's economy averaged 8 per cent annual growth during the 1960s and early '70s, and while much of this was attributable to US expenditure during the Vietnam War years, the Thai government did push economic development, including welcoming foreign investment. There was also considerable national development, with irrigation, electrification and other infrastructure projects undertaken.

In terms of foreign policy Thailand remained staunchly anti-communist and a close ally of the US in fighting communism in neighbouring countries. At home the government fought against communist insurgency, centred primarily in the north-east of the country, and while the state was never seriously threatened (although communist insurgency would not be totally eradicated until 1987), the military effort was draining materially and psychologically, especially when Thai forces were at the same time engaged in the Vietnam War.

Sarit died in December 1963 and was succeeded by his deputy, Field Marshal Thanom Kittikhachon. There was little immediate change and it was not until June 1968 that the drafting process for a constitution, begun eight years earlier, was finally completed. Elections were held in February 1969, with Thanom's United Thai People's Party winning 75 seats in the 219-seat lower house and the Democrats coming second in a 13-party race. However, less than three years later, in November 1971, Thanom staged a coup against his own government, suspended the 1968 constitution, and put executive and legislative authority in the hands of a military junta comprising himself, his deputy, Field Marshal Praphat Charusathian, and his son, Narong Kittikachorn.

The move was an attempt to suppress growing opposition within the military and more significantly among the population at large, especially students, but also workers and business people, with discontent focused primarily on incompetence and corruption within the government and on the Thai alliance with the US. Ironically it was the latter, through its aid and its military presence in the country, as well as other direct and indirect influences, which helped foster a new social and political awareness that transcended the previous confines of the Thai world, which in turn led to mounting frustration and demands for change.

Student demonstrations against the Thanom government received widespread public sympathy and reached a peak in 1973. They began in June of that year when nine Ramkhamhaeng University students were expelled for publishing an anti-government article in a student newspaper. The students and lecturers were later allowed to re-enroll, but in early October another 13 students were arrested on charges of conspiracy to overthrow the government. This lead to a massive rally numbering several hundred thousand students and others, first at Thammasat University, then at the Democracy Monument on 13 October, demanding the release of those arrested and a new constitution. Thanom was

unable to turn the tide against him and the student leaders secured the promise of a constitution within a year. As the demonstrators were dispersing on the following day violence broke out and soldiers fired into the crowd, leaving more than 70 dead and many more wounded. After such bloodshed, Thanom, Praphat and Narong were forced into exile.

The 'Student Revolution' of 1973 was a turning point in Thai history, as significant in its own way as the 1932 Revolution. It represented a new political consciousness and showed that there was now popular intolerance of strong-man authoritarianism, which triggered a revitalized attempt at democracy.

Immediately after the events of October 1973, Dr Sanya Thammasak, rector of Thammasat University, was appointed interim prime minister and charged with drafting a new constitution. Elections were held in January 1975, but with 42 parties in the field, hardly any of them with a clear ideological base or platform of programmes and almost all focused around familiar political personalities, there was no clear winner. Between February 1975 and October 1976 shaky coalition governments were headed first by Seni Pramoj, then his brother Kukrit and finally Seni again.

The most popular move of this brief period of democracy was to secure the withdrawal of US forces from Thailand, which was begun in March 1975. However, aside from the fragility of the democratic coalitions, external factors served to undermine political stability. Notably, communist victories in Laos, Cambodia and Vietnam in 1975 triggered fear among the general population, while sharp increases in oil prices in 1974 had led to recession and inflation.

Polarization between leftist students and workers and rightist big business and the army increased, ending in violence on 6 October 1976. Students protesting at Thammasat University against the return of Thanom to Thailand as a monk were brutally attacked by members of the Village Scouts, Red Gaurs and other rightist paramilitary groups, along with the police. Officially 43 students and two policemen were killed, although the actual number of student deaths was probably much higher.

The violence was an excuse for a military takeover. A new authoritarian government was installed with Thanin Kraiwichian, an ultra-conservative former high court justice, as prime minister. Due to the particularly repressive regime, numerous student dissidents and left-wing intellectuals either went into exile or

ABOVE
General Prem Tinsulanond, prime minister throughout most of the 1980s, is widely viewed as successfully guiding the country from predominantly military rule to a largely civilian-led government during a period that has been dubbed 'premocracy'.

OPPOSITE
Baiyoke Tower II, Bangkok's tallest building at 90 storeys, exemplifies the unprecedented construction boom that transformed the Thai capital's skyline during the 1980s and '90s.

joined the communist insurgents under the banner of the People's Liberation Army of Thailand (PLAT) in the north and north-east of the country. After just a year Thanin was replaced in October 1977 by the more moderate General Kriangsak Chomanand, who promised a new constitution (which as promulgated in 1978 proved to be closer to the 1932 model than the 1974 one) and elections by 1979. By then, however, a faltering economy and concerns over the Vietnamese invasion of Cambodia, which led to border clashes and an influx of Cambodian refugees into Thailand, had weakened Kriangsak's position. In February 1980 he was replaced by General Prem Tinsulanond, Commander-in-Chief of the army.

POLITICAL DEVELOPMENT AND ECONOMIC GROWTH: 1980–2001

The Prem years from 1980 to 1988 can be seen as marking the beginning of the modern era, a time characterized by rapid economic and social development, yet one in which politics, in spite of at times momentous events, remain today still struggling to secure true democracy based upon more than just a government empowered by victory in general elections.

Development towards democracy made progress under Prem. Although a military man, he cleverly balanced the interests of the military and those of the civilian political parties, which were by and large backed by business. A new constitution fused old and new political trends, and while prominent generals were appointed as cabinet ministers, as well as usually being given the top posts at state enterprises, they were expected to govern in line with the popularly elected Lower House. Democracy and economic growth were seen as the best way of defeating communism, and it was Prem who succeeded in ending the communist insurgency in Thailand with the issuing of a general amnesty.

Prem weathered two attempted military coups, in 1981 and 1985, and following elections in 1983 and again in 1986, he secured his position as a civilian politician with a large majority in the National Assembly, which gave rise to his tenure being known as 'premocracy'. However, pressure for proper democracy and a more dynamic leadership was mounting. After elections in 1988 Prem decided, perhaps reluctantly, to retire; following this an elected MP, Chatichai Choonhavan, a former general although now allied with local business, was appointed prime minister.

From then on, with only a few setbacks, Thailand has been a democracy. However, like history, which as they say gets to be written by the victors, democracy in Thailand tends to be defined by whoever wins a general election, and parliamentary dictatorship has been a constant danger.

Changing the face of politics from the late 1980s onwards was not only the trend of democratically elected governments; there was also huge economic growth that altered the context in which politics were played out. While the military has not been sidelined, the basis of power has shifted towards business and 'money politics'. The difference was noticeable in Chatichai's cabinet line-up, which from 1988 to 1991 comprised about 60 per cent former business executives as opposed to military officers, whereas the percentage in the previous cabinet had been only 38 per cent.

In the latter part of the 1980s and into the mid-1990s, Thailand experienced unprecedented boom years. The economy, fuelled by a concerted export drive, the wooing of foreign investment and determined tourism promotion, achieved double-digit growth and doubled in size in just seven years. Additionally, for the first time manufactured goods overtook agricultural products as the leading export items. The social effect of this was a doubling of both the urban population and the average per capita income, with Thailand witnessing the emergence of a true and effective urban middle class for the first time.

Giving concrete expression to such an extraordinary economic performance was the rapidly and radically changing face of Bangkok. In the late 1970s the city boasted only two high-rise properties, the 23-storey Dusit Thani Hotel and the Chokchai office building. By the end of the century there were close to 1,000 high-rises – offices towers, condominiums and luxury hotels – the tallest, Baiyoke Tower II, soaring to 90 storeys. Powering the building boom and massive infrastructure projects was the creation of giant cement and agro-industry companies, along with a host of related industries and businesses accompanied by vastly increased investor activity.

Chatichai's government initially seemed to bode well for a new era of democratization and the start of replacing officials with elected politicians. However, with a fresh emphasis on business and the diminished threat of communism from Thailand's Indochinese neighbours (Chatichai famously talked of 'turning battlefields into market places'), the military felt that it was losing out on budget allocations and traditional privileges. It accused the government of corruption, calling it a 'buffet cabinet' with references to alleged kickbacks from infrastructure projects, and staged a bloodless coup in February 1991 led by Sunthon Khongsomphong, along with Suchinda Kraprayun and other generals of Class 5 of Chulachomklao Royal Military Academy.

Chatichai was deposed and replaced by a military junta that titled itself the National Peace Keeping Council (NPKC). Parliament was dissolved, the constitution was abolished and a civilian, Anand Panyarachun, a highly respected former diplomat and businessman, was appointed prime minister, mainly to dispel fears of a return to full-scale military rule. Anand and his cabinet performed admirably in spite of being under the scrutiny of the military (indeed, major economic reforms were successfully undertaken during this period).

In December 1991 a new constitution was introduced that virtually assured power would remain in the hands of the military regardless of whichever parties were ostensibly in government. This was proved in March of the following year when a general election brought in a five-party coalition, but the leader of the party with the most votes had to withdraw amid allegations of involvement in the drug trade. The military stepped in and the junta leader, General Suchinda, became prime minister in spite of having earlier pledged not to accept the premiership (a cause of his subsequent unpopularity).

Comprising a mix of military men and businessmen, or 'money politicians', Suchinda's government's vow to eradicate corruption and promote democracy rang hollow and met with mounting opposition from pro-democracy groups united under the Campaign for Popular Democracy (CPD) banner, which had wide support among the urban middle class. A deteriorating situation led to mass demonstrations in Bangkok on 17 May 1992. The demonstrators were rallied by the city's former governor Chamlong Srimueang, a staunch anti-corruption campaigner, and demanded Suchinda's resignation. Suchinda responded by bringing in military units loyal to him. Troops fired on the crowd but were unable to disperse the rally. Clashes continued until the night of 20 May, when King Bhumibol, amid fears of more bloodshed, summoned Chamlong and Suchinda to a royal audience, resulting in the latter's resignation. The situation was thus defused, although it is estimated that 40–60 people were killed over the preceding three days of violence.

ABOVE

Anand Panyarachun, a highly respected former diplomat and businessman, was twice interim prime minister in the early 1990s as Thailand struggled to establish a more stable democracy.

Discredited by the events of May 1992, the military lost political ground and for the rest of the decade various political parties jockeyed for power. No single party ever won an outright majority and all governments were coalitions, with smaller parties often switching allegiance in a kind of political musical chairs. Policies and agendas were usually vague, while accusations and counter-accusations of corruption and vote buying were commonplace.

After another interim premiership by Anand Panyarachun, elections in September 1992 brought in a government headed by the Democrats under Chuan Leekpai, with traditional support in Bangkok and the south. Although Chuan was personally more than competent and 'clean' (if somewhat colourless), he lost power in the 1995 elections to a coalition of conservative and provincial parties headed by Banharn Silpa-archa and his Chart Thai Party. Money politics reigned once more, but claims of widespread corruption forced Banharn to call early elections in November 1996. They were won, arguably somewhat dubiously, by former deputy Prime Minister and army commander Chavalit Yongchaiyudh of the New Aspiration Party.

Politics were overshadowed in the following year, when the bubble of Thailand's economic boom burst. In the great crash of mid-1997 over two million people lost their jobs, the baht fell some 40 per cent against the US dollar and by 1998 the economy had shrunk by 11 per cent, ending a 40-year period during which growth had never fallen below 4 per cent per year. The causes of the crash were multiple. They were summed up by historians Pasuk Phongpaichit and Chris Baker as resulting from 'the explosive chemistry' of mixing careless lending by international finance with 'the pirate instincts of Thai businessmen and politicians'.

Under fire from the business sector and the urban middle class for his handling of the financial crisis, Chavalit, after being forced to seek a loan from the International Monetary Fund (IMF), resigned in November 1997, resulting in the return of Chuan and the Democrats following a new alignment of coalition partners. Emphasizing crisis management and economic reform, the Democrats succeeded in getting the IMF to alter the initially harsh terms of its loan package, and painstakingly set about trying to put the nation's finances in order. However, although the Democrats seemed competent in their efforts, their co-operation with the IMF caused much debate about Thailand's independence, the perceived 'neo-colonialism' of the IMF and the preservation of the Thai way of life, which eventually resulted in the collapse of Chuan's government just days before its term was scheduled to end.

THE NEW MILLENNIUM: 2001 TO THE PRESENT

Thai politics in the first years of the 21st century have been and remain dominated by one man, the flamboyant self-made telecoms billionaire Thaksin Shinawatra. History has yet to judge him, but on current showing his principle achievement has been to polarize Thai society. To his supporters he is viewed as someone who challenges the old guard, promotes true democracy and champions the rural poor. To his detractors he is a parliamentary dictator intent on enriching himself, his clan and his cronies, while maintaining mass support through populist policies. This

is history in the making – Thaksin is currently in self-imposed exile, although his influence is far from absent – and no final analysis is yet possible. For present purposes an outline of the major events over the past decade or so must suffice.

Thaksin swept to power when his Thai Rak Thai (Thais Love Thais) Party, which he had founded in 1998, won a landslide victory in the January 2001 elections. Capturing 40 per cent of the vote, more than any previous prime minister in a free election, he was only three parliamentary seats short of an absolute majority. In order to gain total control Thaksin opted for a coalition with the Chart Thai and New Aspiration Parties, while absorbing the smaller Seritham Party.

As one of the country's most successful and richest entrepreneurs Thaksin had the support of big business, but he also cleverly wooed the rural poor, especially in the north-east and north, his home base, who had been mostly marginalized in the recovery from the economic crisis, with such populist policies as universal access to healthcare and a three-year debt moratorium for farmers. He presented himself as a strong leader and blended traditional strong-man nationalism with modern business and technological know-how. Exuding self-confidence, he was seen as a person who could get things done.

ABOVE

Thaksin Shinawatra was Thailand's most powerful prime minister, winning more of the popular vote in the 2001 elections than any previous civilian premier, but since being ousted by a military coup in 2006 and later going into self-imposed exile to avoid a two-year prison sentence for abuse of power, he has become a divisive figure.

Perhaps because of his results-oriented, self-proclaimed, 'CEO-style' of premiership, how things got done did not seem to matter. For example, in January 2003 Thaksin launched a three month-long 'war on drugs'. While this was effective in reducing drug consumption and generally met with public approval, it left an estimated 2,000–2,500 people dead. Officially the deaths were put down to disputes between drug gangs, although human rights organizations claim that they were in fact the result of extrajudicial killings condoned by the authorities.

A similarly heavy-handed approach was used towards an outbreak of violence in the ongoing insurgency (controversial as to its causes) in the country's three ethnic Malay Muslim-dominated southernmost provinces. Among the most notorious incidents, in October 2004 hundreds of Muslim demonstrators were detained at a peaceful protest and packed into army trucks so tightly that 78 died of suffocation. In spite of increased military and police activity in the region, Thaksin made no headway in finding a solution to the southern problem.

On the economic front Thaksin successfully continued the road to recovery and repaid the IMF loan ahead of schedule. By 2002 the economy was once again booming, benefiting not only Bangkok but also rural areas, where various programmes, such as low-interest agricultural loans, infrastructure development, and the 'One Tambon (administrative district) One Product' (OTOP) rural small- and medium-enterprise development, all initially bore fruit. However, there was criticism that many of the rural programmes were unsustainable, creating a dependence on handouts rather than promoting self-sufficiency.

In March 2005 Thaksin became the first-ever Thai prime minister to complete his full term of office, and moreover won a second term with a landslide victory at the polls. In spite of the huge election win Thaksin's government was soon faced with growing criticism, with claims of it being a parliamentary dictatorship in which check-and-balance mechanisms were being neutralized and the media menaced. There was a feeling that big business and big money were taking control of the state by what critics called 'policy corruption' in that, for example, infrastructure and liberalization policies, albeit legal and potentially valid, tended to benefit companies owned by family members and close associates.

The most outspoken critic was Sonthi Limthongkun, a media mogul and host of a TV talk show who aired accusations against Thaksin. When the programme was forced to close he became even more vocal, and in mid-2005 he and

Chamlong Srimueang founded a mass protest movement known as the People's Alliance for Democracy (PAD) – also called 'yellow shirts' after the protesters' chosen dress code – supported by business people and the urban middle class.

The crunch came in January 2006, when Thaksin sold his family's controlling interest in his telecoms company, Shin Corporation, to Temasek Holdings, a Singaporean sovereign wealth fund. The sale, worth some US$1.88 billion, alienated many Thais because it was made to a foreign company and, more galling, because it had been structured in such a way as to be exempt from capital gains tax.

The pace of politics over the following years was rapid, with quickly changing events that were often bizarre and at times violent.

In the wake of public protests calling for his resignation, Thaksin dissolved parliament on 24 February 2006 and called a snap election on 2 April. The election was boycotted by the Democrats and other opposition parties and thus, by the terms of the constitution, was invalid. Another election was set for 15 October but before then, on 19 September 2006, a bloodless military coup overthrew the government, which was accused of corruption, interference with state agencies and creating social divisions. The coup deposed Thaksin while he was in New York attending the UN General Assembly. Martial law imposed a new constitution, endorsed by a referendum in August 2007, which increased the power of the judiciary and weakened the power of elected politicians. Fresh elections were held in the following December and were won, to the dismay of the military and PAD, by a pro-Thaksin coalition led by the People's Power Party (PPP), a reincarnation of the disbanded Thai Rak Thai, with Samak Sunthorawet as prime minister. This prompted more protests and in September 2008 Samak was dismissed by the Constitutional Court for violating conflict-of-interest laws by holding alternate employment – namely appearing on a weekly TV cooking show! Somchai Wongsawat, a former senior civil servant and, incidentally, Thaksin's brother-in-law, was then chosen by parliament as the new prime minister.

Meanwhile in October 2008, ongoing corruption charges against Thaksin resulted in him being found guilty of abuse of power in a land deal whereby he helped his wife buy land from a state agency at a reduced price, and he was sentenced in absentia to a two-year jail term. Since then he has not returned to Thailand, basing himself in Dubai and keeping in touch with his supporters at home via video links and out-of-country meetings.

In late 2008 PAD launched a 'final battle' to topple the pro-Thaksin government and rallied tens of thousands of supporters for mass demonstrations that culminated in a week-long blockade of Bangkok International Airport. PAD was ultimately successful in that Somchai was removed from office in December 2008 after a Constitutional Court disbanded the PPP for alleged electoral fraud and barred its leader from politics for five years. Opposition leader Abhisit Vejjajiva of the Democrat Party then secured a coalition within Parliament and became the new prime minister, the third new leader in as many months.

The impetus of protests now shifted from the anti-Thaksin PAD to the pro-Thaksin Democratic Alliance Against Dictatorship – or 'Red Shirts' in Thailand's colour-coded protest movements – which was founded in 2006 and is supported primarily by the rural poor of the north and north-east. Demonstrations demanding Abhisit's resignation escalated through 2009 and peaked in March–May 2010. Sparking a confrontation was the Supreme Court's ruling in February 2010 that Thaksin had illegally acquired US$1.4 billion during his time as prime minister, which stripped him of half his wealth. Tens of thousands of Red Shirts descended on Bangkok and occupied parts of the city centre, setting up barricades and paralyzing the Ratchaprasong shopping district.

RIGHT

Anti-government, pro-Thaksin 'Red Shirt' demonstrators massed in Bangkok between March and May 2010 and were only forcibly dispersed by the Army after efforts to find a peaceful solution failed.

The Abhisit Government was unwilling to meet the Red Shirts' demand for the dissolution of the Assembly and a snap election, and after efforts to find a peaceful solution failed the army was sent in to disperse the protesters. Ongoing clashes during two months and the final military action left 91 people dead and over 1,800 wounded among the protesters, the military and bystanders.

There are those who argue that the Red Shirts' demonstration was a genuine grassroots call for democracy, while others claim that it was an armed insurrection (so-called 'men in black' among the protesters did have weapons), managed and financed by vested interests. The debate continues, as do attempts at reconciliation and the proposal of various amnesty bills.

A degree of political stability was achieved when the pro-Thaksin Pheu Thai Party won a landslide victory in the July 2011 general elections. Thaksin's younger sister, Yingluck Shinawatra, was appointed prime minister, Thailand's first female leader, although Thaksin himself, still in self-imposed exile, was widely thought to be in control. Society remained divided, and sustained massive anti-government demonstrations in Bangkok in 2013 and on into 2014, with pro-Thaksin supporters rallying on the city's outskirts and sporadic lethal clashes, finally leading to the military, headed by General Prayuth Chan-ocha, declaring martial law on May 20, 2014. This was followed two days later by a full coup and suspension of the constitution.

Previously, Prime Minister Yingluck had been forced to resign following a controversial Constitutional Court ruling, hence the military justified its actions as the only way to restore order and prevent further civil strife. A new government was formed with General Prayuth as Prime Minister and the promise of a new constitution and elections at an unspecified date.

On 13 October 2016, King Bhumibol Adulyadej died at the age of 88, and the nation was plunged into mourning at the passing of this beloved monarch who had guided the country since 1946. He was succeeded by his son who ascended the throne as King Maha Vajiralongkorn Bodindradebayavarangkun, Rama X.

Thailand has the form of democracy, but its practice, effectively addressing the concerns of all social groups, has been problematic and remains elusive. As to the future, there is cause for optimism in the Thais' traditional resilience and capacity for social cohesion, while the equally traditional allegiance to one's clan and a near-feudal system of patronage remain stumbling blocks.

ABOVE
Pictured delivering a speech to the Asia Society in New York on 26 September 2012, Yingluck Shinawatra was elected as Thailand's first female prime minister in 2011.

OVERLEAF
In the last few decades Bangkok has sustained enormous changes, though development elsewhere has been uneven, prompting a growing political divide between the city and rural populations.

APPENDIX
Kings and Prime Ministers of Thailand

SUKHOTHAI

Si Intharaditya	?1238–?1270s
Ban Mueang	?1270s–?1279
Ramkhamhaeng	?1279–1298
Loe Thai	1298–1346/7
Ngua Nam Thum	1346–47
Lue Thai (Mahathammaracha I)	1347–1368/74?
Mahathammaracha II	1368/74?–1398
Mahathammaracha III	1398–1419
Mahathammaracha IV	1419–1438

CHIANG MAI

Mengrai	1259 (1292 at Chiang Mai) 1317
Chai Songkhram	1317–1318
Saen Phun (1st reign)	1318–1319
Khrua	1319–1322
Nam Thuam	1322–1324
Saen Phu (2nd reign)	1324–1328
Kham Fu	1328–1337
Pha Yu	1337–1355
Ku Na	1355–1385
Saen Mueang Ma	1385–1401
Sam Fang Kaen	1401–1441
Tilokaracha	1441–1487
Yot Chiang Rai	1487–1495
Mueang Kaeo	1495–1526
Ket Chettharat (1st reign)	1526–1538

Chai	1538–1543
Ket Chettharat (2nd reign)	1543–1545
Queen Chiraprapha	1545–1546
Interregnum	1546–1551
Mekuti	1551–1564

Under Burmese Suzerainty

Queen Wisutthithewi	1564–1578
Prince Tharawaddy (viceroy)	1578–1607
Sons of Tharawaddy?	1607–1613
Thadogyaw	1613–1615
Si Song Mueang	1615–1631
Phraya Thipphanet	1631–1659
Ruler of Phrae	1659–1672
Ingsemang	1672–1675
Chephutarai	1675–1707
Mangraenara	1707–1727
Thep Sing (independent ruler)	1727
Ong Kham	1727–1759
Ong Chan	1759–1761
Khi Hut	1761–1762
Abhayagamani	1762–1768
Moyagamani	1768–1771

Chao of Chiang Mai

Kavila (at Lampang 1775–1781)	1781–1813
Thammalangka	1813–1821

Kham Fan	1821–1825
Phutthawong	1825–1846
Mahawong	1846–1854
Kavilorot	1856–1870
Inthanon	1871–1897
Suriyawong	1901–1911
In Kaeo	1911–1939

AYUTTHAYA	
Ramathibodi I	1351–1369
Ramesuan (1st reign)	1369–1370
Borommaracha I	1370–1388
Thong Chan	1388
Ramesuan (2nd reign)	1388–1395
Ramaracha	1395–1409
Intharacha I	1409–1424
Borommaracha II	1424–1448
Borommatrailokanat (Trailok)	1448–1488
Intharacha II	1488–1491
Ramathibodi II	1491–1529
Borommaracha IV	1529–1533
Ratsada	1533–1534
Chairacha	1534–1547
Yot Fa	1547–1548
Khun Worawong (usurper)	June–July 1548
Chakkraphat	July 1548–January 1569
Mahin	January–August 1569
Maha Thammaracha	1569–1590
Naresuan	1590–1605
Ekkathotsarot	1605–1610/11
Si Saowaphak	1610/11
Song Tham	1610/11–1628

Chettha	December 1628–August 1629
Athittayawong	August–September 1629
Prasat Thong	September 1629–August 1656
Chai	7–8 August 1656
Suthammaracha	8 August–26 October 1656
Narai	26 October 1656–1688
Phra Phetracha	1688–1703
Suea	1703–1709
Phumintharacha (Thai Sa)	1709–1733
Borommakot	1733–1758
Uthumphon	April–May 1758
Suriyamarin (Borommaracha)	May 1758–7 April 1767

THONBURI	
Taksin	1767–1782

BANGKOK	
Phra Phutthayotfa (Rama I)	1782–1809
Phra Phutthaloetla (Rama II)	1809–1824
Phra Nangklao (Rama III)	1824–1851
Phra Chomklao (Mongkut, Rama IV)	1851–1868
Phra Chulachomklao (Chulalongkorn, Rama V)	1868–1910
Phra Mongkutklao (Vajiravudh, Rama VI)	1910–1925
Phra Pokklao (Prajadhipok, Rama VII)	1925–1935
Ananda Mahidol (Rama VIII)	1935–1946
Bhumibol Adulyadej (Rama IX)	1946–2016
Maha Vajiralongkorn Bodindradebayavarangkun (Rama X)	2016–

PRIME MINISTERS	
Phraya Manopakonnitithada (Mano)	June 1932–June 1933
Phraya Phahon Phonphayuhasena	June 1933–December 1938
Luang (Plaek) Phibun Songkhram	December 1938–July 1944
Khuang Aphaiwong	August 1944–August 1945
Thawi Bunyaket	August 1945–September 1945
Seni Pramoj	September 1945–January 1946
Khuang Aphaiwong	January 1946–March 1946
Pridi Phanomyong	March 1946–August 1946
Thamrong Nawasawat	August 1946–November 1947
Khuang Aphaiwong	November 1947–April 1948
Luang (Plaek) Phibun Songkhram	April 1948–September 1957
Phote Sarasin	September 1957–December 1957
Thanom Kittikhachon	January 1958–October 1958
Sarit Thanarat	October 1958–December 1963
Thanom Kittikachorn	December 1963–October 1973
Sanya Thammasak	October 1973–February 1975
Seni Pramoj	February 1975–March 1975
Kukrit Pramoj	March 1975–April 1976
Seni Pramoj	April 1976–October 1976
Thanin Kraiwichian	October 1976–October 1977
Kriangsak Chomanand	November 1977–February 1980
Prem Tinsulanond	March 1980–April 1988
Chatichai Choonhavan	April 1988–February 1991
Anand Panyarachun	February 1991–April 1992
Suchinda Kraprayun	April 1992–May 1992
Anand Panyarachun	June 1992–September 1992
Chuan Leekpai	September 1992–July 1995
Banharn Silpa-archa	July 1995–November 1996
Chavalit Yongchaiyudh	November 1996–November 1997
Chuan Leekpai	November 1997–February 2001
Thaksin Shinawatra	February 2001–March 2006
Chitchai Wannasathit (acting)	April 2006–May 2006
Thaksin Shinawatra (caretaker)	May 2006–September 2006
Council for National Security	September 2006–January 2008
Samak Sunthorawet	January 2008–September 2008
Somchai Wongsawat	September 2008–December 2008
Chaowarat Chanwirakun (acting)	2 December 2008–15 December 2008
Abhisit Vejjajiva	December 2008–August 2011
Yingluck Shinawatra	August 2011–May 2014
Prayuth Chan-ocha	August 2014–

RESOURCES

Baker, Chris and Pasuk Phongpaichit, *Thailand's Boom and Bust* (Chiang Mai, Silkworm Books, 1998).

----, *Thailand: Economy and Politics* (Kuala Lumpur, Oxford University Press, 2002).

----, *A History of Thailand* (Cambridge, Cambridge University Press, 2005).

Barwise, J. M. and White, N. J., *A Traveller's History of Southeast Asia* (New York, Interlink Books, 2002).

Bowring, Sir John, *The Kingdom and the People of Siam* (Kuala Lumpur, Oxford University Press, reprint 1969).

Chakrabongse, HRH Prince Chula, *Lords of Life: A History of the Kings of Thailand* (Bangkok, DD Books reprint 1982).

Church, Peter (ed.), *A Short History of South-East Asia* (Singapore, John Wilcy & Sons, 2009).

Coedes, G., *The Making of Southeast Asia*, English edn (Berkeley, University of California Press, 1966).

----, *The Indianized States of Southeast Asia*, English edn (Honolulu, The University Press of Hawaii, 1968).

Crawfurd, John, *Journal of an Embassy to the Courts of Siam and Cochin China* (Singapore, Oxford University Press, reprint 1987).

Cushman, Richard D. (trans.) and David K. Wyatt (ed.), *The Royal Chronicles of Ayutthaya* (Bangkok, The Siam Society Under Royal Patronage, 2000).

De Choisy, Abbe (trans. Smithies, Michael), *Journal of a Voyage to Siam 1685–1686* (Kuala Lumpur, Oxford University Press, reprint 1993).

Gervaise, Nicolas (trans. John Villiers), *The Natural and Political History of the Kingdom of Siam* (Bangkok, White Lotus Co Ltd, reprint 1989).

Graham, W. A., *Siam* (London, The De La More Press, 1924).

Hall, D. G. E., *A History of South-East Asia*, 2nd edn (New York, St Martin's Press, 1966).

Keyes, Charles F., *Thailand: Buddhist Kingdom as Modern Nation-State* (Boulder, Colorado, Westview Press,1989).

Ley, Charles David (ed.), *Portuguese Voyages 1498–1663* (London, J. M. Dent & Sons Ltd, 1947).

Loubère, Simon de la, *The Kingdom of Siam* (Bangkok, White Lotus, reprint 1986).

Mason, Colin, *A Short History of Asia* (Basingstoke, Palgrave Macmillan, 2000).

Smyth, H. Warrington, *Five Years in Siam* (Bangkok, White Lotus, reprint 1994).

Syamananda, Rong, *A History of Thailand* (Bangkok, Chulalongkorn University, 1997).

Tachard, Guy, *Voyage to Siam* (Bangkok, White Orchid Press, reprint 1981).

Terwiel, B. J., *Thailand's Political History: From the Fall of Ayutthaya to Recent Times* (Bangkok, River Books, 2005).

Turpin, F. H. (trans. B. O. Cartwright), *A History of the Kingdom of Siam up to 1770* (Bangkok, White Lotus Co Ltd, reprint 1997).

Vella, Walter F., *Chaiyo! King Vajiravudh and the Development of Thai Nationalism* (Honolulu, University of Hawaii Press, 1978).

Wood, W. A. R., *A History of Siam* (Bangkok, Chalermnit Press, reprint, 1959).

Wyatt, David K., *Thailand: A Short History* (New Haven, Yale University Press, 1984).

INDEX

ACKNOWLEDGEMENTS

The author and publisher would like to thank Michael J. Montesano for his invaluable help with the manuscript and maps.

PICTURE CREDITS

All photos copyright Mark Standen except:

Henry Ray Abrams/X01671/Reuters/Corbis p.223; david_addimage/iStock p.207; Kittikun Arngkasai p.133; Anil Kalhan p.94; Asia Society p.229; Ayutthaya-history.com p.76, 97, 98; bbar/123RF Stock Photo p.41; Bettmann/Corbis p.219; Brian Norcross/Flickr p.107; Bridgeman Art Library p.118; brittak/iStock p.230; Heinrich Damm p.99; John Dominis/Getty p.214; enviromantic/iStock p.81; frameangel/123RF Stock Photo p.140; James A. Warren pp.62, 92; justhavealook/iStock p.80; Hans Kemp/Alamy p.228; Tetsushi Kimura p.122; Gordon Knowles/www.Thailand-Delights.com p.134; lakelman p.91; lingkang/123RF Stock Photo p.171; Haru Maki/Alamy p.225; Aidan McRae p.155; National Archives of Thailand and Fine Arts Department: pp.11, 31, 35, 47, 50, 89, 136, 137, 141, 143, 149, 158, 159, 162, 160, 163, 164, 166, 168, 169, 174, 175, 176, 184, 185, 186, 187, 189, 194, 195, 198, 202, 209, 212, 216; photonewman/123RF Stock Photo p.126; Igor Prahin/Alamy p.167; Daniel Ptti p.78; nightskyman/123RF Stock Photo p.90; Rodin Wu p.128; Andre Roseta p.105; Jochen Schlingman/www.asienreisender.de pp.85, 111, 115; Sodacan p.179; C. Joseph Thiessen p.116; Dan Vincent/Alamy p.131.